T0067195

SPRINTING BACKWARDS TO GOD

DUNCAN SHOKO
SINGS-ALONE, ROSHI

BALBOA.
PRESS

A DIVISION OF HAY HOUSE

Balboa Press books may be ordered through booksellers or by contacting:

Balboa Press
A Division of Hay House
1663 Liberty Drive
Bloomington, IN 47403
www.balboapress.com
1 (877) 407-4847

Because of the dynamic nature of the Internet, any web addresses or
links contained in this book may have changed since publication and
may no longer be valid. The views expressed in this work are solely those
of the author and do not necessarily reflect the views of the publisher,
and the publisher hereby disclaims any responsibility for them.

The author of this book does not dispense medical advice or prescribe the use
of any technique as a form of treatment for physical, emotional, or medical
problems without the advice of a physician, either directly or indirectly. The
intent of the author is only to offer information of a general nature to help
you in your quest for emotional and spiritual well-being. In the event you use
any of the information in this book for yourself, which is your constitutional
right, the author and the publisher assume no responsibility for your actions.

Any people depicted in stock imagery provided by Thinkstock are models,
and such images are being used for illustrative purposes only.
Certain stock imagery © Thinkstock.

Print information available on the last page.

ISBN: 978-1-5043-4077-9 (sc)
ISBN: 978-1-5043-4078-6 (e)

Library of Congress Control Number: 2015915079

Balboa Press rev. date: 11/10/2015

"I chose you because you were already a fool."
—Trail Keeper (from 4th vision Quest)

Dedication

To my mother, Altha Duncan,
who gave me pride in being Cherokee

To George Whitewolf
Indian Brother and Teacher

To Priscilla Cogan
Irish-American Wife and Best Friend

To Laura McKelvey and Nancielee Holbrook
Daughters Who Carry The Teachings
To The Next Generation

To Wendy Williams
Sister and Peerless Trickster

They have enriched my life beyond measure.

Contents

Acknowledgments / *xi*
Foreword / *xiii*
Introduction / *xv*

SOUTH / *1*
  I'm Just a Two-legged / *3*
  Coyote Gets His Name / *4*
  The Out of Balance Saga of the No-Name People / *7*
  Facing South:
      The First Vision Quest; Duncan Gets His Name / *12*
  Signs from the Spirits / *17*
  First Sign / *18*
  The Field Goal / *21*
  Deep Water Babtism / *24*
  Fatherhood / *27*
  The Ordination Train Rolling / *33*
  End of the Beginning / *35*

EAST / *47*
  Do Not Think of Them as the Four Directions / *49*
  Coyote and Rabbit / *50*
  Facing East:
      The Second Vision Quest; Donut in the Grass / *55*
  Mini-Enlightenment / *59*
  The Mummy / *63*
  The Temple / *65*
  Moving on Down the Road / *69*
  The Invisible Man / *73*
  Metatantay / *75*
  Rolling Thunder / *81*
  Teachers Everywhere / *90*
  The Mystic Desert / *93*
  That Lecherous Coyote! / *96*
  Horns of a Dilemma / *100*
  Transformations / *104*

How Men and Women Found Each Other / *114*
Committed to Marriage / *119*
Strawberries / *121*
Taking My Bride / *125*
The Lady Dreams / *129*

NORTH / *131*
Facing North:
    The Third Vision Quest; Thunder Beings / *133*
Gun Smoke / *136*
I Will Kill You / *139*
Building Defenses / *142*
Healing / *144*
The Cancer Ballet / *147*
Hospital Feathers / *151*

WEST / *153*
Holy Coyote / *155*
Vision Quest / *165*
Facing West:
    The Fourth Vision Quest; Already a Fool / *166*
Coyote Speaks / *171*
The Shaman's Helmet / *173*
Tatanka Wee Wee / *176*
Grandfather, I Am Going to Drink / *178*
Indians Can't Be Hypnotized / *181*
The Sacred Pipe / *183*
Mom's Lowanpi / *187*
Mid-November / *190*
Full Circle / *191*
The Last Word . . . Maybe / *194*

GLOSSARY / *197*
HYMNS QUOTED / *201*
POSTSCRIPT / *203*

Acknowledgments

My thanks to the Grandfathers of the Four Winds, my Spirit Helpers, and Teachers. Without them this book would never have been written. As a Native American story teller, with humor at the bone, I have culled my memory for stories illustrating how the Spirits have guided my life. The Trickster Spirits, especially, have worked overtime on my behalf.

These stories span many years and so many twists and turns of my life, that it would take another book to acknowledge all those who have helped or influenced me. My deepest appreciation goes to Priscilla Cogan, soul mate and first editor, who demanded my best work; Rolling Thunder, who called me to the Red Road; George Whitewolf, who patiently guided my journey; and to the many Indian brothers and sisters who have honored me with their trust. My gratitude is extended to Lois Beardslee, Native Story Teller and Artist, who perfectly translated this book into a single drawing, featured on the cover. Thanks also to Rosemary Barker for her helpful suggestions, and finally, my deepest appreciation to Elizabeth Gaylynn Baker who helped me remold this work into its final form. Wado! To all of you.

Some individual and place names have been altered to preserve the privacy of innocents. The names of my Spirit Teachers and Medicine Helpers have been changed for such information is not public.

Duncan Shoko Sings-Alone, Roshi

Foreword

When I skip forward, following the light of my dreams and the direction of my spiritual visions, often the gravity of my intent slams my feet solidly back to earth. Hard as I try, the way becomes too difficult, too humiliating to continue slogging onward. It is at those times that I fully suspect that God is laughing at us.

In an act of sheer bravery (or candid folly), Roshi Sings-Alone invites us into those moments of his life journey. His collection of stories clearly illustrates the mirages we create for ourselves by our spiritual hungers, our overactive imaginations. These mirages become a banquet for Coyote, the Trickster Spirit.

What he reminds us in his delightful, humorous tales of tribulation is that Coyote was sent to put us human beings back into balance with the Creation, anyway he can!

Duncan's well-told stories teach us that if we keep our eyes open, if we pay attention to signs, and if we maintain a sense of humor and humility, we will end up learning about ourselves and the ever mysterious Sacred world that surrounds our existence.

So when the forward way to the Sacred becomes impossible, try turning around and walking backwards to God, laughing. At that moment, gravity loosens its grip and we can shake off weighty preconceptions, hone our sense of awe, and fully enter into the heart of Creation. Maybe only then can we truly hear God's laughter.

Priscilla Cogan, author
Winona's Web
Compass of the Heart
Crack at Dusk: Crook of Dawn

Introduction

*I*n the beginning . . .
of the Cherokee Creation Story, all the plants and animals were settled on earth before the first man and woman arrived in the Great Smoky Mountains. Nearly all such narratives, including the Genesis story, agree that human beings were the last created and the most in need of help. From the beginning Grandmother Earth has had to succor us in special ways.

Sometimes our help comes in a Sign. Most western, technological, science-ridden people are blind to Signs, but a bird, tree or event may portend something important. Native Americans expect and watch for them, but also have the wisdom to discriminate. Not every sign is a "Sign." Sometimes the hawk is simply looking for food rather than revealing himself as a medicine animal.

Guiding Signs may also come from the Spirit World. The closest analogy in Judeo-Christian tradition would be the Legion of Angels. American Indians have legions of Spirits, some of whom previously led human lives, but many of whom did not. My own Teacher, who introduced himself during a healing ceremony and revealed himself more fully during my fourth Vision Quest, lived hundreds of years ago as a Lakota.

Spirits can be helpful, provocative, or destructive. There is a constant struggle between Good and Evil Spirits to control human endeavors. Knowing that, Native Americans start every sacred ceremony with a rite of purification and protection. They understand that anything worth noticing will inevitably attract both kinds. All reality is fueled by the interaction of opposites: male/female, positive/negative, light/dark.

Then there is the separate class of Spirits that are neither good or bad. Known as Trickster Spirits, they teach wisdom through foolishness. Exemplified in American Indian stories by Rabbit, Raccoon, Coyote, Raven and Spider, it is Coyote that represents the prototypical Trickster.

Coyote is an incredibly complex fellow; a nere-do-well, sly and cunning, with an avaricious appetite for women. Even when he does good, it is usually in service of his sensuality. Yet, as you will learn in the story, *How Coyote Got His Name*, Creator pitied poor Coyote and empowered him to restore balance to Creation whenever necessary. So that is how Coyote works, albeit in fits and starts. At the Creator's request, he enters our lives whenever we get out of balance.

There is a little Coyote in all of us and a lot of Coyote in some. Truly troublesome, our own human perversity becomes Coyote's best tool. Consider the number of national leaders who have worked hard for the people but allowed lechery, greed, and egotism to tarnish their image and render them foolish. This is the way of Coyote.

Story-telling has always been a great past-time in my family. So it was natural for me to become a story teller. I love the Cherokee legends and animal tales; in fact, stories are my favorite form of teaching. Honed by my life-long teacher, Professor Coyote, I haven't lost my trickster personality. My stories, many autobiographical in nature, may be strange and sometimes embarrassing, but they are always true and thereby important to anyone walking the sacred path. The following stories are from my repertoire of teaching tales which reveal Coyote's meddlesome assistance in my life.

Here then is my personal history, important only as it reflects a chapter of the Creator's story, laid out like a medicine wheel. These stories aren't meant to be taken at face value. As you move along in the four directions, South, East, North and West, unanswered questions may jar your awareness. They certainly did mine. Be patient as each tale discloses its own truth, and meanings emerge from the maze. There are spiritual teachings in even the most unseemly of tales. Each level of learning marks a milestone of my path of vision quest And always remember; regardless of whether we notice it or not, life is sacred, but sometimes we must walk backwards to God.

Roshi Sings-Alone

Dear Reader Beware!
You Are Entering An Illogical and Curvilinear World.
—Coyote

South

The Color is white.

It represents new life, the energy of adolescence,
new learning, and discovery.
We also face South when it is our time to cross over.
Birth and death are the two faces of life.

South is represented by the Elk Nation.

I'm Just a Two-legged

A hau, I am just
A two-legged
Surrounded!

Good Spirits, protect me
From my Ego.
Bad Spirits, stay away.
I know nothing.
Trickster Spirits,
Laugh with me
At myself.

A hau, I'm just
A two-legged
Surrounded!

Good Spirits, teach me
Compassionate wisdom.
Bad Spirits, shoo!
I'll not say Yes.
Trickster Spirits,
Be gentle with me.

A hau, I'm just
A two-legged
Surrounded!

Good Spirits,
You scold me,
Say I'm not
In balance.
Bad Spirits
You promise me
Power that
Boomerangs.
Trickster Spirits,
You trip me
And dab my wounds
With salt.

A hau, I'm just
A two-legged
Surrounded.

—Priscilla Cogan

Coyote Gets His Name

A Traditional Tale from the Northwest Coast

The Creator's last act before colonizing human beings on earth required naming all the animals. Until then the creatures had temporary names. Grandfather commanded all the animals to gather at the next sunrise for a great Naming Ceremony. They might request a new name or keep their old one.

Coyote was ecstatic for he hated his name, Coyote, which means Imitator. No one could possibly value such a name. Coyote bragged that he would head the naming line at dawn. Puffing up his chest, he boasted, "I will be Grizzly, the great warrior. Or maybe I will take the name, Eagle. If per chance the Creator has reserved those names for someone else, then I will be Salmon."

Swaggering among the animals, he boasted that he would arrive first at the Creator's lodge and choose the very best name. "I own the number one spot," he loudly declared.

The animals thought Coyote an arrogant fool. They teased him, "Imitator, you don't qualify for a new name. No one wants your old one, so you will be stuck with it."

"Nonsense", said Coyote, "I will be Grizzly or Eagle or Salmon. You just wait. As first in line, I will demand the name I want!"

Raven mocked him, "Coyote, you're so lazy I bet you won't rise from your bed until mid-morning."

Coyote smiled indulgently, "All right, give me a hard time, but you're looking at the new Grizzly come sunrise tomorrow."

That evening when he returned home, his children were crying. "Daddy, did you bring us food? We are hungry." They crowded around him begging for something to eat.

"Hush, foolish children. Do not bother me with such trivia. Tomorrow I will be Grizzly, the great warrior. Stop whining and go to sleep. Leave me alone. A great warrior requires time to collect his thoughts."

Coyote's wife, Mole Woman, was angry with him but kept out of his way. She could not satisfy hungry babies with the small bits of food she could scavenge. Although Mole Woman loved her husband, she resented his slovenly ways.

As darkness settled, the animals retired to their homes to eat and sleep. Coyote's table was bare because he had spent his time boasting rather than providing for his family.

Coyote did not dare to sleep.

"No," Coyote said to himself, "I must not doze off, or I will oversleep and miss getting my name."

Coyote settled by the fire determined to stay awake and head the Naming line at dawn. As the moon trekked across the sky, Coyote grew drowsy. He pushed tiny sticks between his eyelids forcing them to remain open, but nothing seemed to help. Morning dispelled the night, and fatigue clouded his consciousness.

Coyote slept.

At dawn all the animals but Coyote marched to the Great Naming. Even Mole Woman was there. She had left Coyote sleeping by the fire. Mole Woman feared that if Coyote acquired a grand name he would leave her. In spite of Coyote's foolishness, she loved him and could not countenance losing him. Thus, she stole away to the Creator's Lodge, abandoning Coyote to sleep.

At high noon, Mole Woman returned. As she entered the den, silly Coyote awoke, thinking it was sunrise, and bolted for Grandfather's lodge. Yanking open the door, he confronted the Ancient One. "Grandfather, I want my new name. I shall be called Grizzly," panted Coyote with excitement.

"Sorry, Grandson, that name was granted hours ago. You cannot be Grizzly."

Coyote, though stung by disappointment, pressed his cause. "Well, I didn't really want that name. I prefer to be known as Eagle."

"Eagle was named hours ago, Grandson. I am sorry, but it looks like you must remain Coyote."

"Nooo, Grandfather," Coyote wailed in grief, "If I can't be Grizzly or Eagle, please name me Salmon. I hate being Imitator."

"You should have presented yourself at sunrise. Salmon has already been named. Imitator has been your name and Imitator you shall remain."

Coyote collapsed, humiliated. How could he face the other animals after bragging so shamelessly?

Grandfather felt sorry for poor dejected Coyote and mused, *Surely, I can do something for him.* And so Grandfather pondered deeply. Finally, He proclaimed, "Imitator, because you overslept you must retain your name. Unfortunately, the animals will laugh at you. But, I have work for you to do. I am glad that you came last to my lodge, for you shall be special among all the tribes."

Grandfather continued, "The world remains unfinished. More must be accomplished. There are monsters to be tamed before the Human Beings arrive. You will subdue the monsters for me. Even after the two-leggeds come, where their lives stumble out of balance, you shall be the one chosen to stabilize them."

Grandfather warned, "For all the good works you perform, sometimes you will be praised and honored. But, for all your foolish and mean deeds, you will be derided and despised. Go now; you will have much work to do."

To this day, Coyote remains very proud to be special and while he always endeavors to do good, like many of us he is thwarted by his ego and appetites.

So beware. Coyote lurks nearby to give you a helping hand when your world is out of balance. . . .

The Out of Balance
Saga of the No-Name People

Coyote was traveling in unfamiliar country when he stumbled upon a weird scene. Quickly hiding under a bush, he watched the surreal tableau before him. Animals were behaving in a most bizarre and uncharacteristic manner. Rabbits were attempting to climb trees. Birds were crawling in the dirt. Snakes kept jumping off rocks trying to fly, and a Bear was floundering in the lake. In fact, the big guy would dive under water, stay too long, and break the surface gagging and coughing. Bear had been in the water so long that his fur was sloughing off in bunches.

This is crazy, thought Coyote as he scratched his ear and watched in disbelief. *I have to investigate.*

"Hey Bear! Yeah, you out there in the water. What are you doing?" yelled Coyote.

Bear spluttered, "Well, I'm trying to live under the water, but I can't get the knack of it, and I'm very tired. Every time I fall asleep, I choke."

Coyote waded out into the lake, took Bear by the ears, peered into his eyes and said, "Looky here, you're a bear. Bears don't live in the water. Bears dive into the water for an occasional swim, or wade out to catch a fish."

Coyote lifted up Bear's front leg, "Look at your paw. These claws are for scratching and digging and climbing. If you were supposed to live in water, your paws would be webbed."

"You don't say," said Bear.

Coyote helped Bear out of the lake. It was very difficult for Bear to walk because he had been in the water so long that he wasn't used to carrying his own weight. Finding a shady spot, Bear collapsed on the ground and commenced a long nap.

That settled, Coyote trotted over to the big rock from which snakes were jumping and crashing onto the ground.

"Hey, what's going on?" he asked.

Snake replied, "Sssssssshucks! No matter how hard we try to fly, we just sssssssseem to be knocking ourselves out on the rockssss."

Coyote was nonplused. Patiently, as if talking to a child, Coyote explained, "Snakes don't fly. You're supposed to slither on your bellies. You can move very fast and easy that way. Snakes slither." Coyote wig-wagged his body for emphasis.

"Well, what d'ya know," said Snake. "Sssssseemed to me that sssssomething was wrong with flying."

Snake was delighted to find that slithering was much easier than flying. It was fun to sneak around in the weeds and rest under logs. Soon all the snakes were sneaking and slithering like snakes were supposed to do.

Coyote recalled, "Grandfather warned me that parts of the Creation would be out of balance, but this place is insane. These animals don't know who they are or what they're here for. Good thing I came along when I did, or they would have destroyed themselves by their crazy behavior."

Coyote trotted over to the birds who were crawling on the ground.

"Hey, what you doing down there?"

"Can't you see we are crawling?" said the birds. "We didn't get these broken feathers for nothing. Crawling is hard to do correctly when you are plump like us and have feet which get in the way."

Hawk called out, "Hey, Coyote! Gimme a paw will you? Hold my wing down while I try a wiggle. Every time I try it, a wing pops out and gets in the way."

"Birds! Birds!" yelled Coyote. "Stop a minute and listen. You have it all wrong."

The birds lifted their heads from the dirt.

Coyote continued, "You are birds. Birds are for flying and snakes are for slithering You look as ridiculous trying to crawl as the snakes attempting to fly. Grandfather created you to fly. Flying is your thing."

Coyote grinned, "Try it. You'll like it."

"Well," they replied, "It won't hurt to try." So, the birds began to flap their wings, and soon they were soaring high in the sky. Far below they saw the snakes happily slithering about.

Hawk sang out, "Flying is great! That slithering is for the birds." He chuckled at his own joke.

Coyote was pleased with what he had done, but there was more. Rabbits were still trying to climb trees and squirrels were hopping around on their hind legs.

Group by group, Coyote put them straight. Before he left, he explained who they were and made sure that they knew their names and their purposes. It took a while but when he had finished the job, he was pleased with himself.

Many seasons passed before Coyote returned. To his horror he found bears splashing in the lake, snakes again jumping off the rock, rabbits climbing trees, and birds slithering in the dirt.

Coyote sighed, "Grandfather sure gave me a tough job. These creatures insist on being what they aren't." Going to each animal, Coyote again gave them their names and explained their purposes. As an after-thought, Coyote gave each one a card with the animal's picture and purpose clearly printed on it. Now the creatures were happy and relieved. The cards made them feel safe and sure they would not forget.

Coyote ascertained that all the creatures were settled into their appropriate roles before he departed once again.

A few months later Coyote back-tracked to see how the animals were faring with their I.D. cards. To his dismay and aggravation, the animals were once again confused and in chaos. Their cards had been lost or ruined. Not only would they require more cards, but this time they insisted that Coyote stay with them and become their personal guru.

"With Coyote in residence, we will always know who we are. We won't have to depend on our memories or mere cards," they reasoned.

Coyote explained that Grandfather had made him responsible for many things. He had other demands on his time and could not spend his whole life teaching them things they should already know. No way could he move in with them!

The animals became angry. Coyote had no right to teach them new ways and then leave. His teachings were teasings if he would not stay with them. They complained bitterly among themselves, each group being more outraged than the others. They grew angrier and angrier until with a roar they fell upon Coyote, biting him, beating him, and tearing at his fur.

Coyote feared for his life. Being a quick thinker, Coyote had a revelation. He knew just how to save himself and teach these foolish animals a lesson at the same time.

"Stop! Stop! Hold on a minute," screamed Coyote. "Stop attacking me and I will teach you a great secret. I will show you the source of my magic to know and change things. I will connect you to all the Spirits of Creation. You will be powerful like me."

The animals agreed that this was a fine offer. It was hard playing all those diverse parts. They could never keep straight which was the right role for each group. So if Coyote would share the source of his magic, then each one could become whatever he wanted to be at the moment. What fun to hold the sacred key to power and knowledge! The animals backed off as Coyote struggled to catch his breath while rubbing his bruises and licking his cuts.

After calming down, Coyote sat the animals in a circle. With great pomposity and a solemn expression on his face, he told the animals to lower their eyelids half-mast. Bear was chosen to be the example. Coyote sat him in the center of the circle facing East. Coyote retrieved a beautiful clear crystal from his medicine bag and tied it to Bear's snout so that Bear could see straight down the stone. Coyote instructed Bear to squint and fix his vision a sapling's length ahead.

Coyote assumed his most mystical voice, "Bear, you have a great power that lies coiled just inside your butt at the base of your spine. You foolishly lose the power every day by dumping it on the ground. You must learn to raise the power up your spine, focus it out of your eyes and through this crystal."

Bear tried very hard to understand this teaching. It was obviously of great mystical importance.

Coyote continued, "Now, I want you to relax. This next step is a bit strange but necessary to force the energy up the spine instead of out on the ground. Coyote took a corn cob which had been lying in the soft mud and was very slippery.

Holding the slimy cob up for everyone to see, Coyote said, "Bear, insert this Sacred Stopper in your anus and hold it there."

Bear did as he was told.

"Ooooo," chorused the animals, obviously impressed. They loved sacred things and simply adored obscure rituals.

"It is very important," warned Coyote, "that you not expel the Sacred Stopper during the ceremony. The spiritual energy must rise rather than be wasted on the ground."

Bear concentrated mightily as Coyote continued, "Now, tightly close your mouth and begin to suck in. Act like you are pulling the Sacred Stopper from inside right up to your head. Feel that vacuum? With the Sacred Stopper closing the lower door, you are sucking up your spiritual power. Raise it now! Raise your energy! Raise it! Up! Up! Up!"

Bear tried very hard not to expel the cob. It was uncomfortable to hold it in and sit still too. The Sacred Stopper wanted to come out. Bear sucked valiantly until Coyote was satisfied that Bear's energy was raised and ready.

"Now," intoned Coyote, "gently, gently push . . . not enough to expel the Stopper . . . just a little. Squint your eyes and sight down the crystal."

Coyote waited a bit to let Bear have the full effect of his energy struggling to go down while Bear willed it to rise.

Then Coyote urged Bear, "Push your energy into the crystal. Look for a beam of light . . . look for the light . . . it is beginning to flow. You will see it streaming from the stone."

Coyote paused to indicate that the magic was about to happen. "In the beam you will see a small creature, your personal guide. Remember his face for this is your teacher forever. He will make you just like me."

Another pause and then Coyote whispered urgently (and loud enough for all to hear), "Look intently. . . . Be aware. . . . Look intently. . . . Be aware. . . . Keep your focus."

Sure enough. It was only a short time and a little discomfort before Bear became sure he was seeing something. "Yes! Yes! I see the light. I see the beam." Bear was ecstatic, "It's there. I see . . . I see . . . I see my guide!" Sure enough, Bear had found his personal spirit guide and was tuned into magic, power, and truth.

Coyote, in the meantime, slid off into the bushes and escaped. He paused at the top of the hill and looked back. By now all the animals were tying crystals to their noses and stuffing Sacred Stoppers up their rears. They were ready!

Coyote watched them with a mixture of disdain and pity. He thought to himself, "Those who refuse to be themselves become caricatures of what they imitate."

Facing South: The First Vision Quest; Duncan Gets His Name

1979 – Vision Quest Hill, Whitewolf's Place, Rural Maryland

Involved in sacred ceremonies for several years, the time arrived for my first Vision Quest. I would pray for a name and an understanding of my calling . . . for the work I would do for my people. My identity as a Cherokee was finally clear to me.

Preparation for Hanblecheya involves an intense mixture of prayer, fasting, work, and in my case of course, Coyote mischief. Hanblecheya in Lakota means, "To Cry for a Vision." English speakers named this ceremony, Vision Quest. By late winter, prospective vision questers greet each dawn with a Sacred Pipe ceremony and endure a food fast one day a week. By the last month prior to Hanblecheya, usually in May, supplicants typically fast food and water one day a week, pray with the Pipe daily, and participate in Inipi (Sweatlodge) as often as possible. These activities help make one strong enough to endure the rigors of Vision Questing.

I approached my first Hanblecheya with a mixture of fear and yearning. Meanwhile, Coyote bounced around me and the other novice vision questers, grinning from ear to ear. We heard warnings from Whitewolf and Sam (his Lakota brother), "Look out for Big Foot. She loves to wander through here this time of year. She follows the stream down there and exudes an awful stench. We smelled her powerfully when she passed by last year."

Not being a total idiot, I recognized the fictitiousness of Big Foot, but I knew that the Hanblecheya was serious business.

"Thing is," my tormentors continued, "Spring brings Big Foot into heat. Damn, I hope She doesn't find you out there on the hill all alone."

Another constant caution, "Beware, the black tailed deer. She'll shape shift into a beautiful woman who will whisper to you, 'Why don't you leave your altar and join me in the woods? No one will ever know, and we will have some fun, you and I. Look at my body. Its yours if you come with me.' You must ignore her or she will persist."

Ominously, Whitewolf would add, "If you forsake your altar and go with her, she will lead you deeper and deeper into the woods, until you are lost. Your Vision Quest will be terminated before it ever begins. Even worse, I have heard stories in South Dakota of Vision Questers who disappeared forever, apparently because they were bewitched by the Black Tail Deer Woman. I bet she will come for you."

They pestered me with all the dire warnings and predictions they could muster. "Be ready to die on the hill. That may be your Vision," they'd growl, and this I knew was true. One never went to the hill assured of a safe return. Vision Questers have died during Hanblecheya.

So, I prepared well. This first Vision Quest would require one day and one night, without food or water, with no company, and no human help. Alone with the Spirits and the Creator on a hillside in rural Maryland, I would cry for a vision. I tied one hundred tobacco ties for each of the four directions. These tiny, tobacco-filled, prayer pouches would define the perimeter of my altar. Purchasing a standard legal form, I carefully detailed my Last Will and Testament. Having put my affairs in order, I was ready.

Dawn broke on my Hanblecheya morning in mid-June. White-wolf joined me in my Vision Quest area as we smoked the Sacred Pipe and prayed. Later that morning, the community gathered for my final meal: kidney stew and raw kidney for purification, raw buffalo heart for courage. Then, the men shared with me a quick two-round sweatlodge ceremony.

Finally, holding my Sacred Pipe in front of me, and followed by Whitewolf with the entire community trailing behind, we climbed to the altar area where everyone hugged me "goodbye." They departed, leaving me there quite alone. Unbidden tears filled my eyes. Awed about confronting the Creator, I feared I might not see my friends again.

The altar area extended about 10 feet in each direction bounded by strands of tobacco ties. In the altar rested my Medicine Bundle, Sacred Pipe, a couple of blankets, and an eagle wing fan. Clad only in a Vision quest skirt, I waited.

Those first moments on the hill were excruciatingly lonely. I began to pray long prayers, but I found there is a limited number of prayers one can offer. Within a half hour I had touched on every topic from the local community to foreign lands, from Grandmother Earth to planetary pollution.

Having "prayed out," I began to listen. A light rain kissed my cheeks. Smiling inwardly, I thought, *The air is warm. I can handle this.* As the hours dragged by, I struggled to remain alert.

I remembered all that Whitewolf had taught about Vision Quest. He had said, "Watch everything. Pay attention or your medicine animal might slip by and you would miss it. A Spirit Teacher could stand guard over you and you wouldn't see him. Beware the Black Tailed Deer. You know about her, but also note anyone who materializes by your altar and wants to join you. Nothing evil can enter there unless you break the circle of protection bounded by your tobacco ties." He elaborated, "If someone arrives and wants to come in, point your pipe at him and say, 'If you are a good spirit from Wakan Tanka, come smoke with me. If you are not, depart from here.' Never offer your pipe to anyone just because they ask for it. You must test the Spirits. There are Evil Spirits bent on harming you. Be careful!"

His words resonated ominously of life and death.

The memory of Whitewolf's voice flooded my consciousness, "Any ceremony, particularly a Vision Quest, is like a lightning rod, attracting Spirits from all over: Good Spirits, Evil Spirits, and Trickster Spirits as well. Remember, if you choose to leave the altar, you are blind to what lurks outside. If you must go to the bushes, do it quickly and return to your altar as fast as you can." He showed the way to exit and reenter the altar, the protective power of the tobacco remaining intact. The teachings cycled through my awareness. Careful and alert, my confidence was growing.

"I can handle this," I affirmed.

Toward dusk, I left to relieve myself and then jumped back into the altar for the night. The skies dripped and drizzled, and around the altar the night whispered sounds: foot steps, rustling bushes, clicking noises.

"I can handle this." I was confident.

Hours into the night a sensation began to grow at the edges of my awareness. Finally, located in my bladder, it began to warn, "You're filling up. Before long you'll have to go."

I responded to the pressure angrily, "No way in hell am I leaving this altar in the dark. Unh Unh. No way!"

The moon, totally hidden by the clouds, rendered the night a velvet black. God knows what lurked outside that altar. Maybe the black tail deer was stalking me.

The urge was insistent, "You are either going out there or in here." The warning had grown to a demand. No choice remained but to follow Whitewolf's instructions for creating an altar door. I gingerly stepped into the dark unknown.

"Come on, you. Let's do it and get out of here!" I commanded myself.

It took an age to start and an eternity to finish. Almost feeling the Black Tail Deer's hot breath on my neck, I jumped back into the altar and sealed the door. My "I can handle this," was switching into "I hope I make it."

Songs poured from my soul, spilled out of the altar, covered the hill, and flooded the valley where the community kept vigil. Grandmother honored me with a strong voice whose power increased proportionally to my anxiety. I saturated the night with Four Direction Songs, Pipe Songs, and Sun Dance Songs.

All through the night, the Native American community followed my voice echoing around the surrounding hill tops. Their prayers of thanksgiving echoed their inner relief. "He's doing good. His voice is strong."

When not singing I struggled to remain alert and vigilant. A doe appeared just outside my altar, no, not the Black Tailed Deer Woman, just a white tailed doe. A Bear revealed himself in the clouds. The usual night insects, the mosquitos, and the beautiful night moths visited my altar. For a few tranquil moments, a black butterfly fluttered around my Pipe and the altar area. Except for the bear and deer, nothing else of significance seemed to materialize for me.

Dawn finally broke the hold of night. I thanked the Grandfather Sun for showing Himself again, laid down to rest a while, and was sound asleep when Sam roused me. He led the way down the hill. Holding my Pipe in front of me, I followed triumphantly. The community waited but could not look directly at me for I was still sacred from the Vision Quest. The stones were hot and ready as I entered directly into the sweatlodge.

In this closing ceremony of the Vision Quest, I reiterated to Whitewolf all that happened on the Hill; the night sounds, the clicking, the deer, and the bear. He was told that the clicks were Spirit sounds approving my Vision Quest. Liking my songs, The Spirits named me "Sings-Alone." There is more to the name than that, but I will not publicly reveal it. A spiritual name must not be bandied about. It requires privacy and respect. Sings-Alone is a good name. I wear it with pride. The Spirits foretold that someday I would bring assimilated, urban Indians back to their ancestors, linking traditional Indian people with those who want to reconnect with their ancestral ways.

The Spirits prompted, "Something else happened up there. Think hard." I tried, but couldn't imagine what They were talking about. They insisted that I trace the whole Vision Quest again in my mind. Trying without luck and succumbing to the intense heat, I gave up. I was told that when I remembered the rest of my Hanblecheya to ask about it in the next sweatlodge ceremony.

Every Vision Quest terminates in a Wopila (Feast of Thanksgiving) and a joyful reconnection with the community. Chatting with Whitewolf, I allowed, "I cannot imagine what else the Spirits were talking about. I really saw nothing of importance. There were the usual night insects like the mosquitos and there was this one little butterfly."

He laughed and said, "That was probably it. Tell about your butterfly in the next Inipi."

A week later, hunkered against the steam and blinding heat of the sweatlodge, I described the tiny, black butterfly that had visited my Vision Quest altar. The Grandfather Spirits responded, "The butterfly is an important medicine for you. After the lodge, return to your altar space, fill your Pipe and pray. The butterfly will offer itself to you. Take it and return to Whitewolf. He will show you what to do."

Obediently, I ascended the hill to my altar. Filling my Pipe, I knelt in prayer in the exact spot I had occupied during my Vision Quest. Suddenly, the butterfly appeared, circled my Pipe, and settled facing me on the stem. Thankfully, I took the little butterfly in hand and returned to the community.

I had survived my first Vision Quest without being molested by a female Big Foot, abducted by the Black Tailed Deer Woman, or possessed by an Evil Spirit. And I had my medicine and my sacred name.

Inside, I foolishly smiled, "I handled that!"

In that very moment I failed to hear Coyote's howl.

Signs from the Spirits

For each of us, God holds a plan if we desire to live in a sacred way. I have come to appreciate how actively Good Spirits and Coyote Spirits correct our false starts and direct us to our true fate. In my own odyssey, from a Christian pre-ministerial candidate to a Native American Spiritual teacher, why didn't Creator just stick an eagle feather in my hair and say, "Get thee hence to an Indian teacher and learn from him?" It is only in looking backward that I recognize how often my path was marked by 'signs' I blindly missed. Sorta like this Iowa farm boy:

A farm boy struggled with his plow as he stumbled along behind the old mule. The sun burned his face and neck. Dust clogged his lungs. It had been a long, hard day. Suddenly the letters "P C" materialized in the clouds, an obvious sign from heaven. Throwing down the plow, he raced across the fields to the farm house yelling, "God called me to preach Christ. I saw it in the clouds! It said, 'P C. P C.' Preach Christ! Hallelujah!"
The sign really meant, "Plow corn."
Aho!

—A folk tale, Author unknown.

First Sign

. . . of Something Gone Wrong

I was born into an Anglo-assimilated family in which our Cherokee blood was valued but the sacred teachings and ceremonies were not. My Cherokee mother, a proud minister's wife, and my Christian clergyman father did not denigrate Native ways. The old practices were simply unknown to them.

As a boy, there were two great longings that impelled my dreams and desires: The Lord God, and a Nash Ambassador and not necessarily in that order. I loved God and I worshipped automobiles. My creeds were consistent with those of my Dad: There is but one God and you shall have no other God before Him, and there is but one Nash Ambassador, and you shall have no other car than this.

My father had warned me early that he would never buy me a car. The only exception would be if I were a seminarian and needed transportation to rural, student parishes. Little did he realize in that moment, unwittingly, that he had handed me the means to satisfy my two most powerful needs! I could serve God AND get a car. What else could my twelve year old mind do but choose the ministry?

Murky motivations are the way of Coyote. Had I had the slightest idea or desire to read or follow signs, I might have saved myself much time, money and embarrassment, but I would have missed my life. There were things I had to learn along the way, and Coyote was a class A teacher.

My father was a great man and a respected minister. His life work transformed the world around him. As a man who stood for principle, he grew to legendary proportions in my mind. I admired his personal courage and strength of character. So, I chose the ministry for my life's work. Of a spiritual bent from birth, this appeared the appropriate choice, but of course, one doesn't simply 'choose' to be a minister. There must be a "Call," a special event that clearly signifies that the individual was chosen by God.

I was missing the "Call."

My determination to get that Call made me a perfect foil for old Coyote. He became my primary tutor.

1948 – Eighth Grade Summer Camp

For many adolescents Church Summer Camp is a marvelous time of play, study, and spiritual awakening. Seventh Grade Camp came and went without my receiving divine notice for the ministry. There was still hope for me. Eighth Grade Camp was coming. This had to be my time.

Each day began and ended with all the campers standing and holding hands in a large prayer circle. Friday night marked the last evening of church camp. It was also the time when God would most likely extend the "Call" to the worthiest campers. A six-foot wooden cross stood sentinel before a large paper-mache earth. A spot-light, judiciously situated, illuminated the cross and sent its shadow falling upon the globe. The symbolism was obvious and impressive enough to shiver the heart and mind of any adolescent waiting for God's signal.

That night a reverent group encircled the cross and paper-mache planet. This was it. I either got the call tonight or would have to hang on yet another whole year. We stood, waiting expectantly in the dark warm night. Suddenly the spotlight flicked on and the shadow of the cross traversed not only the globe but also fell across this hopeful, eighth grade, wannabee minister. This was my sign! God was saying, "I want you in my ministry."

Youthful voices began to sing,

> "This is my Father's world,
> And to my list'ning ears..."

High holiness and sanctity were flooding my soul as I prepared to step forward. Suddenly the grounds-keeper's Weimaraner dog galloped into the center of the circle, legs prancing, ears flopping, and teeth locked onto something in its great jaws. In the dim light we could barely discern a squirming armadillo trying to escape. In stark fascination, we watched as the predator turned his prey belly up and disemboweled it with one juicy crunch.

The song continued as camp leaders studiously avoided the bloody, life and death battle raging in the center of our circle. Seventy-five adolescents tried to maintain holy decorum. It was an impossible task. Our spirits wanted to laugh while our stomachs wanted to vomit.

It may not have been all that I desired, but it was enough of a "Call" to count. It was also a powerful Sign completely doomed to be ignored. From that day onward, despite the clear picture of both blood and gore, I was aimed for the Christian clergy.

The Field Goal

1956 – Student Parish, Frisco, Texas

> *"A small town has one red light, two grocery stores, three filling stations, and four whores,"* (Charlotte Pugh Burn, Arkansas Storyteller).

Frisco, Texas had no red light at all.

It boasted a population of 600 souls, served by four churches, three clergymen, and one overwhelmed seminarian. The First Christian Church (Disciples of Christ) had "called" me to be their pastor during my three years in seminary. Fear, dread, anxiety and excitement saturated my wife's and my migration to this tiny town where I would learn my trade.

It was a student parish. God must have a special place in heaven for such congregations. These patient folk suffered the platitudinous preaching of young men who passionately divulged answers to questions no one was asking. After all, these seminarians had just achieved their baccalaureate degrees. Thus, imbued with omniscience, ideological fervor, a license to preach, and an audience, the novice preachers felt impelled to infuse their parishioners with enlightenment. Graciously the people endured and, through their tolerance, shaped generations of clergy.

But, misery flowed both ways. The first weeks in a new parish tax even experienced ministers. In our case, the parsonage suffered from old age and neglect. The porch sagged from door to ground. The sink periodically required draining by garden hose when the ancient plumbing clogged. I would learn as much about maintenance as about pastoring here.

Every church member owned the parsonage and voiced opinions about the questionable skills of the young preacher and his wife. Notes were compared about our excessive use of electricity and the wretched state of the lawn. My wife was closely scrutinized for her aptitude as lady of the manse. We knew our lives would not be easy, but on that first day in my first parish I was not prepared for what lay in wait. Signs! Signs! Signs! But, of course, I ignored them all.

We were unpacking the car when old Brother Smith called, "Thank goodness, you are finally here. Nellie Jones is in the McKinney hospital. The old lady is blind and dying. She needs a reverend. Please go to her right away."

To tell the truth, I was scared to death, totally intimidated. I had never before made a pastoral call. I knew nothing of death and dying. I felt much too young to be taken seriously by the hospital staff, let alone an aged saint, looking for spiritual sustenance in her final hours. Nevertheless, donning my Sunday suit and taking Bible in hand, I sallied forth determined to impress the nurses and patient that I was truly a minister on official business.

It was an old hospital, dull gray and dirty white. Wide cement steps ascended to sun-bleached oaken doors. Surely there was a back entrance for frail patients. Only the fit could climb so far. Once inside, cavernous spaces threatened to swallow my small courage. Awed by the big, empty lobby, I located "Information" and discovered that Sister Jones was in Room A153.

Corridor A must have been the length of five football fields. My footsteps echoed around me as I negotiated the endless hallway, holding my breath past the nurses' station, sure that every nurse tracked me with suspicious and disapproving eyes. It was a long, miserable trek to Room A153. Once there, I timidly opened the door.

Nellie Jones, still and corpse-white, lay on her back asleep, as oblivious to the spiritual care descending upon her as I was to the Sign about to crash upon me. On the floor beside her bed stood a receptacle which looked incongruously like an old-fashioned milk bottle. A rubber tube snaked from under her blanket into the bottle.

With a deep breath and a silent cry for Divine help, I faced the bed, my head and heart in pious rush toward Sister Jones. Surely my legs and feet would follow.

Any fool could walk to the bedside of a terminal patient, read a psalm, offer a prayer and leave. No special training is mandated. Ordination is irrelevant. Walk, read, pray, and go home. Simple! Simple unless a furry paw, hidden under the bed, surreptitiously inches a urine collection bottle toward an unwary foot.

In a football game this would have been a three pointer from the thirty-five yard line. A great kick! The urine bottle careened off my toe and arched in slow motion toward the opposite wall, rubber tube flapping obscenely behind it. Sister Jones exploded from her nap and shrieked straight up in the bed, her blind eyes raking the dark. Doubtless, she had never experienced a catheter being removed so decisively.

And she never knew who did it.

Turning without a word, scriptures unread and prayers unsaid, I fled the room and retraced my journey up Corridor A with as much speed as my demolished dignity would allow. Scarcely slowing a step, I suggested that a nurse check on room A153.

The right Reverend went home, never to return. Sister Jones died the next morning. My first pastoral act was a success only if you count the field goal.

Deep Water Babtism

I don't know about today, but back in the 50's every country church in Texas held an annual revival meeting. A big-time preacher was hired for a week of evangelistic services. It was a great social time as people visited from all the neighboring churches. There was fervent preaching, generous offerings, rambunctious gospel singing, socializing, pot luck dinners, and a determined assault on those hold-outs who had never been "saved."

Most everyone in town belonged to a church. The revivals reaped an annual harvest of children who had come of age and spouses who had married into the community, but few of the diehard unsaved ever surrendered. Our small rural town of Frisco boasted four churches whose annual revival meetings rendered four weeks of serious attention to these holdouts. They would receive at least one home visit by the preacher and the evangelist and perhaps more from dedicated laymen. In a place where monotony was the norm, such singular attention might be the high point of their year. Why should the "unchurched" give up their unique status?

My first week in Frisco coincided with the annual revival. Our revival produced eight new members needing baptism. There were five children, two adult women and one man scheduled to be baptized Sunday evening at the revival's climax. Our denomination, like the Baptists, dunked the whole body under water. It was said that my father would hold a baptismal candidate submerged while checking to be sure that no errant hand or foot escaped the holy bath. One could never be too careful.

My baptistry was a small tank of water about five feet deep. There was a portable stool on which the children could stand. One by one the candidates would be led down the steps into the pool and positioned carefully so that there would be room to lay them back in the water.

The sacred text would be recited, the individual dunked and then led from the pool as the next candidate entered.

It would seem to be an easy process, but it is not. There are several approved techniques for baptizing converts without half-drowning them. Fat ladies float. Lay them back in the water and their feet will rise, leaving the ladies no choice but to flap their arms like refugees from the Titanic, splashing water . When this happens the pastor loses all possibility of decorum, and the ceremony takes on the character of a cat fight.

Proper technique directs the left palm to be placed firmly under the candidate's chin as the fingers squeeze shut the nose. The left elbow should press down on the chest to keep the feet and lower part of the body down. The right hand cradles the back of the head and the right elbow supports the upper back and shoulders. I mentally rehearsed the process.

Having never performed the ritual, I was determined to produce a flawless baptismal service. Sunday afternoon my wife joined me at church where I practiced dunking her again and again. Her purity thereafter could never be questioned. If one baptism would save you, multiple baptisms had to make you a saint.

Sunday evening, the evangelist was in rare form, and the service unfolded smoothly until it was time for my pastoral "redemption." A few moments were required for the baptismal candidates and myself to prepare. Robes replaced clothing and nervous giggles were stifled. I feverishly pulled up my waders (the kind trout fishermen wear), pulled down my black robe, and descended into the pool. A slow, mournful hymn of many verses afforded adequate time to complete the preparations. As the congregation finished the final "Amen," the candidates and I were ready.

First came the children who were baptized without a hitch. I was gaining confidence by the moment. Then came the first woman. No problem. The second lady was a bit "fluffy" and proved to be a floater, but with my left elbow planted firmly between her breasts, she remained grounded. Only one more baptism and the ordeal would be finished.

Unfortunately, Coyote's visit was imminent as the sole man entered the tank. He was six feet six, considerably taller than I, thus nullifying all my calculations about wedging and support. I decided to compromise by holding his face and nose in my left hand while supporting his shoulders with my right. He seemed to be correctly placed in the pool, so I first raised my hand in blessing, then clamped shut his nostrils while laying him back into the water.

Totally miscalculating the depth, I smashed his head under water upon a concrete step. He jerked, stiffened, and partially collapsed. "Oh shit!" I muttered under my breath. I yanked him out of the water. Two deacons assisted him to the dressing room and laid him on a bench to recover. The congregation thought his rolling eyes and limp knees signified an act of God. I wondered if he realized it was the fumbling of an inexperienced and unholy spirit. I blocked from my mind the very idea that it might be a Sign.

> "Blest be the tie that binds
>   our hearts in Jesus' love.
> The fellowship of Christian minds
>   is like to that above.
>
> We share our mutual woes,
>   our mutual burdens bear;
> and often for each other flows
>   the sympathizing tear."
>
> —John Fawcett

Fatherhood

1957 – Frisco, Texas

Rose and I had met on the first day of classes, our freshman year in Texas Christian University. She was the most lovely, dedicated, Christian girl I had ever known, and she was committed to full time Christian service. We married in September of our Junior year, boasting that she would receive her diploma pregnant, and the baby would be born during my first year in seminary. But no matter how hard we worked at it, she failed to conceive. The work itself wasn't all that difficult, but to no avail. Throughout the first year of my internship in Frisco, we ached for conception; all Rose got were menstrual cramps. Each month, her period levied another bout of depression. We were desperate for a child.

Our local physician, fresh out of medical school, was eager to help. He ordered me to collect a sperm sample which he placed in a slide under his microscope. He invited me to look. Under the stark eye of the microscope the perverse sperm refused to move. Only one or two demonstrated any interest in swimming. Maybe they recognized the futility of trying under those circumstances, but the young doctor pronounced them dead as tadpoles in Clorox. Without live sperm, I obviously could not father children.

Rose and I cried together and railed at the Creator's unfairness. How could we minister to families if we had no family? Day after day, we wallowed in hopelessness until our depression degenerated into boredom. Finally, accepting fate, we determined to reconstruct our dreams by converting infertility into an advantage. In what ministry of the church would childlessness be a boon? The mission field. There would be no unexpected pregnancies to complicate our work in primitive assignments far from medical care. But, if a regular ministry was unacceptable to the Spirits, the prospect of my being a foreign missionary must have lit a real fire in heaven.

For us there was a certain glamour in being missionaries. We would live in exotic places with aboriginal people. Periodically, we would return home to the accolades of adoring church members.

We could even adopt children. The Seventh Day Adventists in the area provided succor to unmarried, pregnant teenagers. Girls would alibi a lengthy visit to Grandma's, which in truth was a special church-run home for unwed mothers. The home facilitated the adoption of the teenagers' babies, and we fit the profile for adoptive parents. When we applied for an infant, we found that a young woman was already in the Adventist Home, and we would be first in line to adopt her baby.

Completing all the necessary applications with the Foreign Missions Board, we expected to be ready for assignment upon my graduation from Brite Theological Seminary. To my dismay, I discovered that choosing to be a missionary was not tantamount to becoming one. The Board had stringent screening procedures, among which was extensive psychological testing.

I sailed through the first day of screening, having no trouble with the I.Q. and other tests administered by a psychological associate. The second morning I encountered the "real" psychologist. This woman was the epitome of intrusive formality. I had barely settled in my chair when she placed before me a bizarre series of inkblots suggestive of sexual activities, violence, and weird animals. I was determined to hold nothing back. I detailed all my perceptions, even the sex organs and explicit, aberrant behaviors. As a psychology undergraduate student, I had heard of the ink blot test but had not expected such gross images.

I had hardly recovered from the visual assault when she commenced her evaluative interview which consisted of the most onerous interpretation of my motives. She labeled me a control freak. She hinted that I yearned to father the world. She accused me of harboring a neurotic need to save humanity. She hinted at an identity crisis. She was right but had no idea of the extent or nature of that crisis. The Spirits could have told her had she been open to Them. Had I been more open to Them I might have acknowledged the truth in her statements. I might have guessed that such accusations were commonly leveled at prospective missionaries. She was testing to see how I would respond to personal criticism. I kept a cool head but was seething inside.

Under the psychologist's attack, missionary work faded as an alternative to live birth. Based on what she said, I assumed I would be rejected. I also questioned whether I wanted to work under a Mission Board which would employ such abusive screening. Maybe we were too hasty in abandoning hope of having our own children. When nothing else works, there is always prayer.

Thus, I chose to visit the meditation room at the Seminary and beseech God for a miracle. I wanted Rose to bear our own child. Without His mighty intervention, she would remain barren.

The meditation room boasted the finest technology of 1957. A panel of buttons could select and play pre-recorded hymns. Another button would activate an intercom arrangement whereby selections from the meditation room could be piped into the seminary chapel. The room was wired so that even words spoken in the meditation room could be broadcast over the chapel PA system. Such an arrangement might provide spectacular special effects, sometimes quite unexpectedly. Of this hookup between the meditation room and seminary chapel, I was totally ignorant.

The seminary chapel, reserved for college convocations and special religious events, occupied a prominent place on campus. Several times a year highly regarded preachers were invited to address the seminary, providing the visiting clergy with opportunity to demonstrate homiletic prowess. Hopefully, the guest minister would return home with renewed vigor to raise money for the Divinity School. Everyone was a winner. The preacher earned honors and the school reaped a windfall. It was on such a morning that I chose to beg God for a baby.

The service began with a formal procession. Vested faculty filed into the sanctuary followed by the Dean and the preacher of the day. The mighty pipe organ thundered its processional march. Seminarians turned to admire the honored clergyman who, wreathed in dignity, was barely managing to contain his enthusiasm. The Dean, himself, presided over the service.

Keeping my appointment for private fertility prayers, I chose not to attend chapel.

After the liturgy was read and introductions presented, the visiting minister ascended the great pulpit. Like a fighter climbing into the ring, he was ready, adrenaline pumping. The moment swelled with righteous dignity. The congregation trembled in expectation.

Completing a few lighthearted remarks and expressing his appreciation to the Dean, the preacher of the day launched his homily. A powerful speaker, he waxed eloquent, jowls shaking with mighty effort. His voice rose and fell in shuddering crescendo and soft admonition, "Moses divided the Red Sea, and Jesus cast out the Gadarene Demoniac. The modern church dares believe nothing and expects little, but God awaits the fervent prayers of the faithful to demonstrate His mighty works in a darkened and evil world." This valiant pulpiteer not only fired up the seminarians, he had the very hosts of heaven taking up arms among the clouds. This was a man of faith. It was an hour of power.

It was also Coyote's time to shine.

I had innocently chosen that very moment to pray in the meditation room, unaware of the glorious spectacle taking place in the chapel. Closing the door behind me, I knelt before the altar. The meditation room was small, cozy, and secure, inviting private communication with the Creator. Thinking that some music might help, I studied the instrument panel beside me. I pushed a button. No music. After a moment, I chose a second. Still nothing. Finally, I touched one that worked. The quiet strains of "Sweet Hour Of Prayer" filled the room and unbeknownst to me, the Seminary Chapel. Coyote style, I had gotten a two-for-one.

> "Sweet hour of prayer! Sweet hour of prayer!
>   That calls me from a world of care,
>   and bids me at my Father's throne
>   Make all my wants and wishes known."

The nonplused preacher stopped, confused, took a deep breath, and charged ahead, determined to override the music. Blissfully ignorant of the fact that I had hit the button which played the hymn in chapel, I had innocently pushed a second button which would have an even more devastating effect.

Red-faced and arms waving, the preacher yelled above the music, trying valiantly to compete, when without warning he was confronted with a fervent prayer in process. An earnest voice implored, "Puleeze God, let my sperm live and swim strongly upstream."

> "Sweet hour of prayer! Sweet hour of prayer!
>   Thy wings shall my petition bear
>   To Him whose truth and faithfulness
>   Engage my waiting soul to bless."

That did it! The guest minister turned toward the Dean, motioned helplessly, and sat down defeated, while the seminarians struggled to smother their laughter.

The Dean charged off the podium and sprinted for the meditation room, yanked open the door and yelled, "Get out! Now!"

I couldn't imagine what caused such violent agitation. Only later, and with great pleasure, did my fellow students enlighten me.

From then on, the Dean could never conceal his dislike and distrust of me. He must have thought it unseemly to pray for live swimming sperm. He suspected that I lacked sufficient dignity for the Cloth; he couldn't picture me in the pulpit. The Dean would as soon eject me from seminary as from the meditation room, but I was an excellent student and came from a respected church family. The poor fellow was stuck with me.

Honest prayer is always heard whether you pray in a Temple, Chapel, or Sweatlodge. God's pity was aroused and Rose conceived. The town shared our joy as her pregnancy changed everything. We dropped our missionary applications, the adoptive child was reassigned, and we awaited the birth of our baby. In a separate part of the same hospital where I endured my first pastoral failure, I experienced my first paternal success. Vicki Sue was born.

A year later when we desired a second baby, I returned to the Meditation Room. The PA system had long since been disconnected so the seminary chapel was safe. I begged God for another child and nine months later our second daughter, Renae, arrived. We were ecstatic at our second miracle. Thereafter, we agreed to practice responsible contraception. A recent seminary graduate, I could ill afford more children.

Three years later, Rose became pregnant again, this time with Laura. We were grateful for another beautiful daughter but determined to be extra careful from then on. We could afford three children, but four would overtax our resources. We laughed at the doctor's diagnosis and gratefully acknowledged the power of prayer even as we came to suspect a faulty sperm analysis.

Two years later, Rose conceived again. We couldn't turn off the pregnancies. Dead sperm? Hardly! We were elated with the birth of our son, Paul. I had given up hope of having a boy to carry on the family name and treasure our male traditions.

But enough was enough. I had a vasectomy.

Before our second child was born, I had completed seminary and received my Divinity diploma. A lifetime in the Christian ministry awaited me, but neither the Good Spirits of the Creator, the Trickster Spirits of Mr. Coyote, nor the Dean was happy with my candidacy for ordination. The Dean worried I might reflect poorly on the Divinity School and the Spirits had other plans for my life.

Stubborn as a mule, I would not be deterred from my course.

The Ordination Train Rolling

1959 – Cedar Crest Christian Church, Dallas, Texas

S heer grit and determination has its rewards. Despite clear signs and warnings to the contrary, I had completed my pastoral training and stubbornly amassed the academic credits necessary to graduate from seminary. The Trickster Train was rolling and ordination was the next stop. No one dared to suggest that I was riding the wrong train. My ticket was punched and the train groaned toward its destiny.

Perhaps the Spirits were amused watching this mixed-blood Cherokee become a minister of the gospel. After all, nothing about being Cherokee precluded one from the ministry. There were numerous Cherokee pastors. The problem was with this Cherokee.

At ordination the Spirits tried one last time to derail the train. But when all the switches are locked, the engine cannot be shunted to a siding. My switches were frozen in a conception of reality ignorant of Signs. My train chugged full speed ahead.

It was an evening service and I was the sole ordinand. The congregation waited expectantly. Senior Clergy sat wrapped in their dignity. An older pastor, friend of both my father and myself, bisected the kneeling rug from his ordination and gave half to me for my ceremony. What a beautiful gift. The bishop, called a general minister in my denomination, presided. This was my moment.

Unbeknownst to me the litany of ordination paralleled the Spirits' own private liturgy. Macro-clear signs of negative import were pending. The words of Samuel Stone filled the church as congregation and organ struggled through the hymn:

> "The church's one foundation is Jesus Christ her Lord;
> she is his new creation by water and the word.
> From heaven He came and . . ."

Out of the auditorium's twilight a shadow shuddered toward the altar. At first the intruder fluttered at the edges of awareness, then horrified the bat-phobics by banking and wheeling in the air like a miniature fighter plane gone amok. Women swatted at their heads in panic. Ushers rose to attack the beast with brooms and rolled bulletins as the bat frantically pursued its kamikaze mission. All the while, clergy, choir and a few valiant congregants stubbornly continued the hymn,

> ". . . sought her
> to be His holy bride.
> With His own blood He bought her,
> and for her life He died."

Finally, an heroic usher batted down and disposed of the little critter. I felt incredible relief and deep gratitude for the saint that preserved us from the creature of the night. After a few moments the congregation calmed down, and the ceremony draped itself once again in appropriate solemnity.

For another ten minutes or so the service flowed smoothly toward its denouement. Spirits said, "Let's give it one more shot."

Suddenly, without warning, the lights dimmed, flickered, and disappeared throughout the church, the only building in the community to lose power. Once again, gasps rippled through the congregation, punctuated by the scurry of feet as the ushers fumbled for the circuit breakers. The liturgy stopped cold. Uncertainty lay like a silent mantel over the congregation. Nothing was happening or about to happen in a darkness pierced only by the flickering light of two altar candles. They cast mystic illusions in the blackness but were totally inadequate for reading the liturgy. This was not a night of good omens.

A small, timid flame materialized. The Bishop, rummaging beneath his robes, had conjured wee magic. He flicked his BIC. Other lighters were passed to the altar and the liturgy lurched forward once again. Periodic grunts punctuated the dignity when overheated BICs burned fingers as the ceremony slouched toward its finish.

The Trickster Spirits had tried their best to derail the ordination, but this time They failed. Their clear warnings about my "Calling" had been treated by me as bizarre coincidences. In the cozy womb of a church, accompanied by a bat, a shroud of darkness, and a host of BICs, I was anointed a full fledged Reverend.

End of the Beginning

I f the sperm prayer piped into the chapel had not alerted me to divine disapproval, nothing but hard experience would. Ordained and fully commissioned, I assumed the controls of my first real parish. No longer able to hide behind the role of intern, I was now fully responsible for my ministry. The Spirits had done their best to stop me, but undaunted, I arrived in my vaunted position of Christian leadership. My stubbornness seemed to grow in inverse relationship to my intelligence.

For the next eight years, I vainly struggled to fit my Cherokee soul into a Christian minister's mold. Truth to tell, the only subject in Seminary that I nearly failed was Theology which, seemed to me, answered questions no one but theologians would ask. Yet, those years in the pastorate were not wasted. Through paranormal experiences the Spirits set out to initiate me into the world of sacred power where the rules of ordinary physics were set aside.

Amos Craft, an obese dandy who dressed impeccably and smoked a big cigar, was a banker and member of my congregation. Carefully coifed, blond hair framed his head. His small, blue eyes peered nervously from deep in his chubby face, belying his carefully sculpted persona of invincibility. Wearing the finest, hand tailored suits and exuding arrogance, he commanded attention. I had no idea about his competence, but if being obnoxious made one a good banker, he was among the best. I failed to recognize that such extreme selfcenteredness can hide a great emotional wound.

His wife sang in the choir. One evening he came early to retrieve her from choir practice. Sitting in the nave of the church, he pulled out a cigar and lit up with no consideration of the singers or the sanctity of the building. One of the feisty, elder ladies of the choir ordered him to remove himself "right now!" Disgusted by his lack of respect, I thanked her.

Having already prejudged him as uncouth and ill mannered, I held no affection for the man. Yet, one afternoon a message, "Call Amos," echoed obsessively in my mind. No matter how I tried to divert my attention, the voice insisted, "Call him!"

That evening as I returned home, I told my wife that I had to phone Amos. She questioned, "Really? Why?"

"I have no idea," I said. "The suggestion to call him keeps churning through my head, driving me crazy. I have to do it."

Opening the directory, I located his office number and dialed. Unexpectedly, I dropped into a private telephone conversation between Amos and his wife. No busy signal prevented me from becoming a third party to their words. Amos was telling her goodbye. He had just taken a drug overdose in his office and was explaining to her that he could no longer tolerate living. Weeping, she begged him not to leave her. His voice, trembling between sobs, assured her of his love, but it was too late. He had swallowed a lethal dose.

Breaking into this morbid conversation, I said, "Amos, stay right where you are. Don't leave."

"Duncan! Is that you?" he cried. "Why are you with my wife?" His voice was tinged with paranoia.

"Amos, I'm not with your wife. Something kept telling me to contact you, and I'm calling from the parsonage. It's a miracle that I got both of you instead of a busy signal." They were stunned into silence.

Hanging up on them, I dialed the rescue squad which raced to Amos's office and found him dazed and staggering down the steps. Hospitalized, he survived the suicide attempt. Later, we marveled together about the miraculous telephone intervention and agreed that, for wh atever reason, the Creator wanted him alive. In the sacred world, crossed wires often spark the miracle of new beginnings. Although the Spirits kept shoving me away from the ministry, They sometimes used me to good ends: a few successes to counter my mistakes, a bit of honey in my jar of flies.

Soon after, They dragged me into the world of Spiritual healing. My liberal denomination looked askance on "faith healing," content to leave such superstitious behavior to Pentecostal churches. But healing work confronted me in a powerful way I could not ignore.

Mark came to our congregation from a church in which a premium was placed on active participation in worship where people might pray

"Amen," cry "Hallelujah," or speak in unknown tongues. Faith healing through the "laying on of hands" highlighted many of their worship services. An active man in his 40's, employed as an auto mechanic, Mark was unconcerned about theological niceties. When he married, he joined his new wife in my parish.

Everyone liked Mark. His sense of humor and lack of pretension put people at ease. Unfortunately, soon after joining our church he suffered a massive heart attack. The prognosis was grim. I rushed to the hospital. I could barely hear him muffled by the oxygen tent .

"Rev. Duncan, doesn't the Bible say that when you are sick, to call the elders and they will heal you?"

"Yes, it does," I replied. Opening my Bible, I read,

> *"Is anyone sick? He should call for the elders of the church and they should pray over him and pour a little oil upon him, calling on the Lord to heal him, and their prayers, if offered in faith, will heal him, for the Lord will make him well; and if his sickness was caused by some sin the Lord will forgive him."*
>
> (James 5:14-15; The Living Bible)

He gave a wan smile and said, "Bring the elders."

I felt a knot in my stomach. This was a service I had never performed as my denomination had no ritual or tradition for it. What kind of oil does one use? 30-weight or "3-in-1?"

Driving directly to the rectory of a friend, an Episcopal priest, I explained my dilemma. After enjoying a good laugh at my expense, he told me to use olive oil. He also provided me with a Prayer Book containing a healing service.

Next, I had to convince my poor, beleaguered, lay elders that they should participate in a faith healing. Announcing that there would be a quick meeting of elders after the morning service, I gathered the wary gentlemen into my office.

"Fellows," I began, "You know that Mark has had a massive heart attack and may not survive. He is still in the hospital with twenty-four hour care."

They nodded in agreement, unsure of what this had to do with them. Everyone knew of Mark's illness.

"Well," I continued, "Mark has asked that the elders come and pray for him under the authority of the Book of James." I read them the verses and added, "I want all of you to meet me back here at three o'clock this afternoon, and we'll go to the hospital and do a healing service."

Looking at each other with bewilderment, they spoke as one, "What do you mean?"

"The Bible tells believers that their elders can heal them, and they have a right to ask," I explained.

It took a few moments, but they all agreed to do their part. In my experience with the church, this was the finest, most dedicated, group of elders I have ever known. Practical fellows, they were not educated in theology. One was a land surveyor, one was a postman, another drove an oil truck. But these men believed and were serious about their responsibilities. So, when I asked them to do something entirely new to them, a healing service, they were willing to try.

Arriving at the hospital we descended on Mark's room in our most serious demeanor. In one hand I clutched my Bible. In the other, a bottle of extra virgin olive oil. It seemed to me that for a healing service the more virginal the oil, the better.

Mark was too weak for pointless chatter, so positioning the elders on either side of the hospital bed, I marked a cross in oil on his forehead. Then we simultaneously placed our hands on his head, maintaining the touch while I specifically prayed for his strength and healing. An electric charge passed through our hands, a tingling sensation. Mark felt it too. Our task finished, we left the hospital without further conversation. Quietness reigned in the car as we each pondered our experience.

In two days, Mark was sent home from the hospital, and in less than two weeks he returned to work.

That was the beginning of my fascination with the immediate experience of spirituality rather than its theological permutations. Searching for other Christians interested in the same things, I discovered an interdenominational group, The Spiritual Frontiers Fellowship. Made up mostly of clergy with a liberal sprinkling of freethinking lay people, the SFF explored all forms of paranormal and spiritual experiences. I became acquainted with a growing cadre of clergy involved in spiritual healing. Convinced that the Bible endorses faith healing, I initiated weekly healing services at our church.

If the Spiritual Frontiers Fellowship represented one end of spiritual practice in the nineteen-sixties, Episcopal Bishop James Pike and the "God is Dead" theologians represented the other. Pike had come to the clergy after a successful career in another field. Progressing rapidly through the ranks, he was soon elected Bishop. It amazed me that a man who apparently believed so little could have attained such an exalted position. His intellectualized religion seemed to me devoid of a direct experience of the Holy. Then, came an amazing transformation in his spiritual consciousness.

While traveling abroad, Pike's son tragically committed suicide. Bishop Pike suffered enormous grief. Struggling to make meaning of the tragedy and overcome the loss of a son, Pike sought out the medium, Arthur Ford. The Bishop became convinced that he could communicate with his son through Mr. Ford. It stood to reason that if he was communicating with his son, then the son had to be alive in another dimension. Forced to accept the concept of an after-life, the Bishop's whole approach to theology was altered.

The Jacksonville Chapter of the SFF arranged for Arthur Ford to do a seance for us. Reluctant to attend, my head warned me against going but my curiosity demanded satisfaction. I signed up. No doubt the Spirits had another lesson for me. On the following Saturday morning, sixteen clergy met on a sun porch of a house overlooking the St. John's River in Jacksonville, Florida.

It was a cool Fall afternoon as the sunlight filtered over us. Wicker chairs and a few folding seats had been placed strategically facing an empty couch. I waited with a mixture of apprehension and eagerness. Most of us had brought our tape recorders. Only two or three of us had previously attended a seance. A nervous covey of clergy settled in to wait for Arthur Ford.

After about fifteen minutes he strode rapidly onto the porch, greeted us perfunctorily, lay down on the couch, covered his eyes with a bandana, and relaxed while we all looked at each other, unspoken questions in our eyes. Ford was about as personable as a coat rack.

I watched his body intently as he moved into a death-like stillness. After several moments Ford jerked slightly, a ripple of energy moving up his body. He coughed a couple of times and began to speak in a deep voice with a pronounced Acadian accent, "People on the other side are gathering. They want to see what we are doing here, and some have come because they have had a relationship with you sitting on the porch."

Ford had little prior notice of which SFF members would attend. I secretly questioned his legitimacy but also realized that he lacked the time or resources to research us. Whatever would come in the seance would result from the mix of participants on both sides of the veil.

Then, the conversations began, the dead speaking through Ford and reminiscing with the living about shared events and concerns. We were amazed as subjects were broached which had been long forgotten. A Methodist minister reconnected with a deceased Presbyterian clergyman he had known years before. They had been in the same town as young men and had shared early experiences in the pastorate. They had argued over doctrinal differences. In awe we listened to the Presbyterian in the Spirit World mention old, private debates. I was sitting there, a wide-eyed voyeur, until Ford spoke,

"That man over there, Duncan."

"Yes," I stammered, my voice caught in my throat.

"Your Grandmother, Polly, is here and wants to speak with you."

"I'm sorry, but I don't have a Grandmother by that name," I said.

"She's another generation away than a Grandmother . . . a Great Grandmother, and she just wants to visit with you."

I was adamant, "I'm very sorry, but I don't recognize the name."

"OK, then, you have an uncle over here, Frank. He wants to say hello."

I was becoming flustered. Uncomfortable being there in the first place, I was suddenly getting unwelcome attention from ghosts I did not recognize.

"Sorry," I repeated. "I don't have a deceased uncle by that name. My mother was an only child and my father had no brothers, just one sister."

"Generations are more important on your side. Sometimes, we say uncle and it could be a great or great, great uncle."

"Well, I am real sorry, but I don't know a Frank."

Arthur Ford grumbled and turned to someone else. I settled back to regain my composure. Ford had agreed to a one hour seance. The time was passing quickly. Although fascinated, I was ready for it to be finished. I personally didn't want any more contacts from the Other Side.

Finally, Ford said, "The power is getting weaker now. I am nearly finished. . . ."

I breathed an inner sigh of relief. This would be a great story to tell, but I was ready to go home.

". . . but before I go I have a very important message for Duncan."

I swallowed hard, sat up straight and replied, "Okay."

"There is a young man here. He has just come over. He died a tragic and unexpected death. His father is a minister in your denomination, a Reverend McAndrews in Tampa."

I searched my mind for the name but could not place him. I did, however, know of the church. Surely, Ford wouldn't ask me to contact McAndrews!

Ford continued, "The boy wants you to tell his father that he is here."

"What do you mean," I replied.

"Call his father and say that the boy is here."

"You want me to call a colleague I don't know and tell him that I met his son here?"

"Yes, it is very important. Will you do it?"

"I don't think so. What would I say?"

"Just say that his son is here."

"Nothing else?"

"That's all. Tell him his son is here. Will you do it? It is important for him to know."

"Okay, I will call him. I don't know how, but I'll do it."

Ford, coughed softly, began to stir, and finally sat up on the couch. Saying he needed to be alone to gather his thoughts, the medium rushed from the room, leaving us to process the seance. My mind was buzzing. How could I honor my commitment to call a man I had never met? Several of the guys teased me about my dilemma. Frankly, I had not a clue about what to say to the grieving family.

Needing to get away and think about what happened, we bid each other farewell and headed for our respective parsonages. All evening I regretted my agreement, but could not renege on my promise to a dead boy, so eventually I repaired to my office. Sitting at my desk, I stared a long while at the ministerial directory. Finally, with the number in hand, I took a deep breath and dialed the Tampa parsonage. The Reverend McAndrews answered.

"Reverend McAndrews," I began, "This is C. W. Duncan. We have never met but I am a ministerial colleague of yours. Not giving him time to respond, I pushed ahead, wanting to get this over with. "I don't know how to explain it, but I was in a seance tonight with Arthur Ford, and he claimed that your son was there. Did a son of yours just die unexpectedly?"

McAndrews' voice had a hard edge, "Yes. He was killed in an accident last week."

"According to Arthur Ford, your boy wants you to know that he is there. I asked if he wanted me to say anything else and he said, "No, just assure my parents that I am here."

McAndrews was not happy with this call. His voice was bitter as he said, "Thanks" and slammed down the receiver.

Coyote had a beaut with that one. How could I know that my Bishop was with the McAndrews family at the very moment of my call? The next week I got a furious phone call from him castigating me both for attending a seance and passing on the suspect message to a bereaved family.

What could I say other than, "I promised the boy I would call." My protest didn't help my plight, but doors in my own mind had been opened that would not close. The world was more complex than my church would admit.

Months later I played the Ford tape for my skeptical father. He nearly fell from his chair when my great-grandmother, Polly, and my great uncle, Frank, were mentioned. Grandma's name was correct, I just did not know it. My great-uncle, Frank, had been a shunned family member, a black sheep whose name was never mentioned.

About nine months after the seance I met Rev. McAndrews at a clergy conference. He rushed up to me, shook my hand, and asked if I was the one who had telephoned about his son. He apologized for being so rude at the time. He told me that the call turned out to be a gift. His wife had been so bitter over her son's death that she had denounced God and felt the afterlife was a hoax. The boy's simple message, "Tell my parents that I am here," made all the difference. Sadly, the McAndrews' appreciation did not mollify the Bishop who continued to accuse me of bad judgement. The lessons I was absorbing in the journey toward my Indian identity overwhelmed me. Each disaster pushed me closer to my exit from a church which distrusted my "superstitious" behavior.

Friend Coyote and Arthur Ford weren't finished with me yet. I finally decided that the ministry was inconsistent with my own spiritual calling. Soon I chose a parish which would allow me to enroll in graduate school to pursue a doctorate in Counseling Psychology. One year into my doctoral program and two years after my first encounter with Arthur Ford, the Spirits arranged a new challenge.

A young couple in their mid-thirties, Tom and Barbara, were very active in the church along with their children. Tom worked hard to provide a good living for his family. They decided to take a vacation in the Great Smokies. Their excitement was contagious. The Cherokee historically inhabited the Smokies. As a mixed-blood visiting my mother's ancestral homeland, I had explored all the mountain parks and camp grounds and was eager to offer suggestions of places their whole family would enjoy.

Then, a week before they were to leave, Barbara began to have frightening premonitions. The trip felt ominous to her. She confided her irrational fears to me with tears in her eyes. Tom thought her intuitions were foolish, some kind of a "woman thing." So, in spite of her dread, the family loaded their vintage station wagon and departed on their long-planned vacation.

A call came in mid-afternoon. Sobbing uncontrollably, it was Barbara saying there had been an accident. A car driven by a drunk had broadsided them. She and the children suffered minor scrapes and bruises, but Tom was dead!

Distraught with grief, Barbara was floundering. My heart cried for her. She faced incredible problems in restabilizing her family and helping her children adjust to their father's death.

As weeks passed, Barbara harbored a secret. She felt Tom constantly hovering about her. Fearing that she was experiencing an incipient psychosis, she was afraid to tell anyone. In a way it was comforting to feel his presence, but it also unsettled her for she had no understanding of what it meant. Her religion had failed to prepare her for this. Finally, crying piteously, she confessed her secret to me, "If only I could speak to him, I would tell him how much I love him and miss him."

Having dared to confide in me, she reminded me periodically that Tom still shadowed her. One Sunday morning Barbara stayed behind after the congregation had left. She faced me with pleading eyes, hands twisting a knotted handkerchief. "Rev. Duncan, I can't stand this much longer. Do you know of anyone who can tell me for sure if Tom's spirit is still here? I have to know."

I had read in the Spiritual Frontiers Fellowship newsletter that Arthur Ford would be lecturing in Jacksonville, Florida. It had been a couple of years since my initial experience with Ford, and I hadn't had contact with any of the SFF people since moving to my current parish.

I told Barbara, "There's a famous medium, Arthur Ford, who will be in Jacksonville next Tuesday evening to give a lecture. If you want, I will take you there, and maybe you can meet him and schedule a seance." I further cautioned her, "Don't get your hopes too high. He tends to be booked solid when he comes to town, but perhaps he will agree to see you."

"I would like that," she said. "At least I have to try."

The following Tuesday we made the seventy mile trip to Jacksonville, found the auditorium, and settled in among the crowd waiting for Ford to appear. There must have been five hundred people present. No one knew we were coming. We spoke to no one after we arrived, and we were hidden in the back of the assembly hall. Ford had no way of anticipating my presence in his audience.

After the typical introductions, he began his lecture. The man remained as colorless as he was on the sun porch in Jacksonville. He was droning on about the Spirit world when suddenly he stopped, put a hand against the side of his head. Frowning, with head cocked to one side, he made a show of listening. The audience was aroused. Expectant. Then, he nodded and said, "There is someone here in the audience whose name is Duncan. He is a student at the University of Florida."

I began to slide down in my chair.

Ford repeated, "Will Duncan raise his hand? I have a very important message for him."

Whether it was intimidation, curiosity, or a combination of both, I slowly lifted my hand.

"Oh, there you are," intoned the great medium. "Dr. Smith has a message for you. He just died unexpectedly, out of the country. He was a cancer researcher at your university, and he wants his colleagues to know that he has been on the wrong track. Will you please pass that message on to them?"

I promptly replied, "No, I will not."

Ford was taken aback by my vehemence. "Why not?"

"I am a doctoral student. If I were to pass along such a message, I might get booted from my department. I will not do it." That was my final word.

Resigned to my emphatic rejection, Ford returned to his lecture and I relaxed. After the meeting, Barbara tried to speak with him, but he would talk with no one. However, being with people who accepted the reality of spirit communication had helped her.

Back in Gainesville the next morning, I hurried to my office, looked up Dr. Smith's number in the university directory and dialed his office.

A secretary answered, "Dr. Smith's office."

"May I speak with Dr. Smith please," I asked in my most professional tone.

"Oh. You must not have heard," she replied. "Dr. Smith was returning from an oncology conference in Tokyo two days ago, had a heart attack, and died on the plane."

I replied, "I am terribly sorry. What an incredible loss." Hanging up, I took a deep breath, thought momentarily about the message and decided to forget it. No way would I jeopardize my standing with the University.

Later, I was admitted to the doctoral program. The time approached for my final qualifying exams. One evening the phone rang and the department chairman said, "Duncan, if you pass we would like for you to become an instructor in the department. You will also be my administrative assistant." What an incredible relief and challenge. I dared not fail the exam. With a guaranteed income I could now escape the ministry.

Qualifying exam week and two days of solid writing loomed on the horizon. The closer the exams approached, the less I knew. On the first day as I sat at the harsh, wooden table, the exam packet sealed before me, I was convinced that I would fail because I couldn't think of any question I could answer. My mind was a blank. A box full of pens mocked my burgeoning amnesia. Deep breathing did not help.

On signal, I opened the exam to the first question. It might as well have been Greek. It made no sense at all. Closing my eyes, I took a couple more deep breaths trying to relax. This time, I could decipher the question. I began to write. Fortunately, once I started, my memory returned. By the end of the second day, the exam was finished.

Then, came the long wait. My exam had to be evaluated by several faculty. The process seemed to take forever. I joined the small cadre of doctoral aspirants sweating the outcome. So much depended on my passing. I not only would be admitted as a formal doctoral candidate, but I would also have a job. It would mark the first time in the department's history that a pre-doctoral student would be granted an instructorship.

When the chairman called to congratulate me and welcome me on board as a faculty member, I was jubilant. With glee I handed my resignation to the Church Board chairman giving sixty days notice.

On my final Sunday, the Bishop, himself, delivered the sermon. He was careful not to gloat over my leaving but was probably delighted. I am sure all the angels in heaven and the Spirits of Wakan Tanka joined the celebration. The service ended, I hung up my vestments for the last time and said goodbye to the Christian ministry. The Spirits finally had Their way.

The next couple of years blurred in frenetic activity; teaching, publishing, and partying. Freed of the church's inhibiting effect, I became a full-time playboy. Embroiled in the Coyote Spirit and with no sense of identity or spiritual anchor, I floundered in unwise relationships and destructive behaviors. My wife enrolled in the College's Department of Educational Psychology, pursuing her own personal dreams. Both of us charged ahead in different directions as our life together became untenable.

In 1971 we divorced.

East

The Color is yellow.

It represents wisdom, knowledge and understanding.
To use the power of the East
is to see with the eye of an eagle
and to perceive the Sacred Hoop
within which we live.

East is represented
by the Eagle.

Do Not Think of Them
as the Four Directions

To where the sun slips into the darkening earth
Casting long night streaks across the sky
    The hawk wheels in lazy spirals
    In search for the jumping mouse.
The sacred mountains yield their mystery.

        My soul is drawn.
        My heart beats fearful.

To where the chilling wind ascends
From subterranean caves and hidden springs
    The old man waits,
    His contemplation done,
His death a forethought, the crystal hall his birthplace.

        The hardness of my logic
        Answers the softness of my love.

To the breakening dawn which bathes
This world in a golden light of forgiveness
    And promises visions
    And promises the new day
The birds sing their songs of renewal.

        The spirit dances in gladness.
        I am a virgin once more.

To where all petals and blossoms turn
In the tracking of the sun
    The arms of man upraised
    In celebration and praise
And life grows rich and luscious and green.

        The heart opens to receive
        And the soul pours forth.

—Priscilla Cogan

Coyote and Rabbit

A Combination of Traditional Tales

R abbit was blithely trekking down the road when suddenly, jerked upside down, he was caught in a trap. The hunter chuckled as he stepped from behind a tree and loomed over his prey.

"You," he boasted, "You're going to be my supper."

Poor Rabbit, slung over the hunter's shoulder, was hauled through the woods to the hunter's cabin and tied securely to a board leaning against the lodge. The hunter filled an iron cauldron, placed it on the fire, and snarled, "When that water boils, in you go, Heh Heh."

Rabbit began to sweat. He tried slipping out of the rope, but no matter how he stretched or twisted, he was tied too tightly to escape. An old woman stomped out of the house with an armload of vegetables. Throwing them on a cutting board, she sliced up the potatoes, celery, carrots, and onions and scraped them into the cauldron. Turning, she appraised the rabbit, smiled hungrily, and returned to the house.

Rabbit groaned in desperation.

Have you ever sensed a presence behind you before you were consciously aware it was there? Rabbit felt someone staring at him and turned his head to see Coyote grinning foolishly close by.

"Hey, Rabbit, whatcha doin?" inquired Coyote.

Now Rabbit was a quick thinker and a glib talker as well, "I had some incredible good luck, my friend. I was walking down the road and these wonderful people invited me to their lodge. They want to do a give-away, so they had me rest on this cradle board while they prepare me a feast. In a little while I am going to have the meal of my life."

Coyote was dumbfounded, "Golly, I sure wish something good would happen to me sometime." His stomach growled at the idea of food, "I'm hungry and nobody ever gives me a feast." He kicked at the dirt.

"Yeah, me either," replied rabbit, "but I stumbled into this. I was at the right place at the right time."

Rabbit shot Coyote a sympathetic glance, paused for dramatic effect, and announced, "I have a brilliant idea. I'm not really hungry, and I have a lot to do. Why don't you take my place and you can have the feast?" He added, "Then I can be on my way doing my errands, and you can feed that empty belly of yours. These people won't care. They just wanted to have a give-away and would as soon feed you as me."

"Naw," said Coyote. "I won't horn in on your good luck, I just wish I'd get lucky sometime."

"Nonsense," assured Rabbit, "Come on. Take my place. I'm not hungry and you are, and these people won't care."

"Are you sure?" said Coyote.

"I've never been more positive about anything in my life," Rabbit hurriedly answered.

"Okay then," rejoiced Coyote, "I'll do it."

Rabbit directed Coyote to untie him. Putting Coyote against the board, Rabbit bound him snugly to the "cradle".

"See ya later," said Rabbit.

"Thanks, Rabbit," responded a grateful Coyote.

Soon, the water was boiling and the hunter, paying no attention, grabbed Coyote by the scruff of the neck and pitched him into the pot. Coyote struggled to escape but the hunter held him down. Just then, the old woman emerged from the lodge, saw what was happening, grabbed Coyote, yanked him up, and plopped him on the ground.

"I won't have that mangy coyote in my soup. What's the matter with you!" she scolded her husband.

Coyote lay in the dirt, confused and angry. Half his hair had been boiled off. Steam wafted off his body. A nasty thought started forming in Coyote's brain, "I wonder if Rabbit did this to me on purpose?" Scrambling to his feet Coyote vowed, "I'm going to find out," and took off after Rabbit's scent. As luck would have it, he discovered Rabbit stretched out in the road about a mile away. Rabbit, lying on his stomach, was holding a small stick in his hand.

"Rabbit, I want to talk to you," growled Coyote.

"Shush! Go away and leave me alone."

Coyote showed his fangs, "Leave you alone nothing! I want to know what happened back there. Those people tried to make a meal of me, not give me a feast."

"Be quiet," warned Rabbit. "Can't you see I am baby-sitting?"

Coyote was hooked, "Baby-sitting what?"

Rabbit replied, "Baby field mice. Mamma and Daddy field mouse had to run some errands and I promised to baby-sit."

"Really?" Field mice were like Hershey Bars to Coyote.

"Yes, I'm to lie here, and if the babies wake up and start to crawl out of that hole, I'll take this stick and gently push them back inside until Mamma and Daddy come home."

Hungry, Coyote plunged into the trap. "I want to baby-sit too!"

"No, go away and be quiet," shushed Rabbit.

"I want to baby-sit. I intend to baby-sit now!" snarled Coyote.

"Oh, all right then. I have better things to do. Lie down here, take this stick, and keep the babies in the hole. Mamma and Daddy will be back before long."

With that, Rabbit departed, leaving a deliriously happy Coyote to take care of the field mice.

Coyote was anything but quiet. He wanted those babies to stir and venture outside. First, he banged the ground in front of the hole, but no babies emerged. He put his mouth over the hole and howled a long coyote howl. The babies did not wake up, but something sinister began to rouse angrily deep inside the hole.

When he could wait no longer, Coyote took the stick and reached far into the back of the hole. Coyote, stretching all the way up to his shoulders, began to scrape the babies out.

Too late poor Coyote discovered that it wasn't baby field mice in the hole. It wasn't a field mouse den at all. Instead, fifty thousand yellow jackets swarmed out from the ground nest and attacked Coyote's hairless behind. Coyote bolted, slapping and howling for the creek. He plunged under its cooling waters. Lying on his back with yellow jackets floating away on the current, Coyote was sure that Rabbit had once again played a dirty trick on him. Rabbit may have bested Coyote so far, but not for long. Rabbit would now pay for his pranks. Nobody made a fool of Coyote!

Coyote tracked him to a pasture where Rabbit was carelessly nosing around. This time, Coyote was cunning. Very carefully he stalked Rabbit until with a single pounce, he captured him. "Gottcha, ya

little twerp! Now it's my turn and you're going into MY stew pot."
Triumphant, he "owned" Rabbit. What a sight they were: Rabbit hung
awkwardly over Coyote's shoulder, Coyote swaggering, his hairless and
bitten behind shining in the sun, his swishing tail looking more like
that of a possum than a coyote.

Back at his lodge, Coyote securely tied Rabbit's feet together and
hung him upside down from a tree limb. Then Coyote lit a fire under
his own water filled stew pot and settled back to wait. Upside down,
Rabbit watched helplessly from the tree.

It would take a while for the water to boil and Coyote was tired. He
had suffered through a difficult day, boiled by the hunter and bitten by
yellow jackets. A little nap before dinner would feel just right. Finding a
nice warm place by the fire, Coyote snuggled down, closed his eyes. . . .

"Whoa!" He was no fool. Once he closed his eyes that sneaky Rabbit
would try to escape. Coyote needed to sleep but also needed someone
to keep an eye on dinner.

Lifting his tail, Coyote commanded, "Anus! Pay attention to that
Rabbit. I'm going to take a nap. Keep your eye on him and if he tries
to get away, wake me up!"

"Frrrrrrrp!" Anus agreed.

Coyote turned around several times like coyotes do, settled down,
moved his tail aside so that Anus could see, and went to sleep. Rabbit
waited until Coyote was deep in slumber. Then, Rabbit began to twist
and turn and loosen the knot.

"Frrrrrrrrrrp"! shouted Anus. "Frrrrrrrrrrrrp!"

Coyote stirred and trained one eye on Rabbit who had suddenly
grown still. Coyote returned to his nap, and Rabbit began to struggle
once again.

"Rrrrrrrrrp . . . . . . .Rrrrrrrrrp!" Anus was frantic.

Coyote opened both eyes, checked on Rabbit who was again
motionless. Coyote sank back into his dreams.

Rabbit had one foot out. He was escaping.

Anus fairly screamed, "Blarrrrrrrrrrrrp! Blarrrrrrrrrrrrp!
Blarrrrrrrrrrrrp!"

Too late, Coyote snapped wide awake, staring in disbelief at the
dangling empty rope.

Twisting around so he could look Anus in the eye, Coyote snarled,
"I thought I told you to watch Rabbit for me. You let him escape."

Anus shrugged, "Flupp."

Coyote snatched a stick from the fire and furiously jabbed it directly into Anus' eye. And that is why Anus is still puckered today, and how Coyote learned the hard way that it is important to pay attention to Signs.

Facing East: The Second Vision Quest; Donut in the Grass

1980 – Whitewolf's Vision Quest Hill, Rural Maryland

During the Wopila (Thanksgiving Feast) following my first Vision Quest, I asked Whitewolf if I might Vision Quest two days and two nights in the early Fall. Still proud of handling my first Hanblecheya with comparative ease, I was ready to ascend the hill again. Splendid visions were undoubtedly pending next time.

Whitewolf smiled but ignored my request. He preferred Hanblecheya in the Spring and early Summer when the earth was blooming with new life. Besides, one Vision Quest a year was plenty. It requires a full year to assimilate all the learning of a single Hanblecheya, and I needed to experience the importance of patience. Perhaps Whitewolf guessed that my next Vision Quest would be a lesson in persistence.

Early Spring the following year found us Vision Questers preparing for the ordeal once again. Each year an additional day and night would be added to the Vision Quest until finally, one might complete four days and four nights.

Typically, Vision Quests were aborted due to lightning, sickness, mosquitos, or other small disasters. It never crossed my mind that such a calamity might terminate my Hanblecheya. I prepared a new Will and listened to the old warnings about the Black Tail Deer Woman. Somehow, the amorous Big Foot was relegated to first time Vision Questers. Tobacco ties were finished. I was ready. "I can handle this!"

My early June Hanblecheya morning began with the usual Pipe Ceremony. The sun shone clear and the temperature was perfect as Whitewolf and I raised the Sacred Pipe in thanksgiving and petitioned for guidance and a "good time." A Lakota, praying for a good time during ceremonies, asks to suffer . . . but suffer well, to experience enough pain to test him, but to suffer no more than he can endure. Frankly, I was never long on "good time" prayers, found no joy at all in pain, and fervently desired to survive the ordeal as comfortably as possible.

Once again the community escorted me to my Hanblecheya altar, hugged me goodby, and disappeared down the hill. I opened my bundle so that it could bathe in the sunlight. Even before I finished organizing my altar, beads of sweat were popping out on my face, back and belly. Grandfather Sun promised to be merciless.

No clouds protected my altar from the sun. Whereas my first Vision Quest was overcast with long periods of drizzling rain, this Hanblecheya would test me with celestial fire. One hour into the afternoon I was burning alive. Grimly, I determined, "I can handle this." Two hours later I was in trouble. Confined to a ten foot square, naked with no shade, escape proved impossible. The sun pounded me into the ground. By nightfall huge doubts clouded my mind. "What if I can't handle this?"

But dusk bathed me in merciful coolness. The night creatures serenaded me and I sang back. The smoke from the camp's sweatlodge fire wafted over the hillside reminding me that the community was in vigil, fasting, praying, and supporting my Vision Quest.

The night eased by swiftly. I dreaded the long second day. Too soon I was chanting the dawn songs, and Grandfather Sun beamed down with nary a cloud for relief. A prescribed sequence of prayers gives a stabilizing structure to the supplicant. Careful to execute the rituals properly, I was determined to persist in my Hanblecheya despite the scorching heat.

Lying on my stomach I studied the ants. My awareness descended beneath the grass into the insect world. A lively place, all manner of bugs pursued their agendas aimfully. I could not always discern their tasks, but the insects moved with sure purpose. My burning hindside jerked me back into the human world. Sitting up, my head throbbed as the hillside began to spin. After a moment the spinning slowed but the throbbing remained. Struggling to my feet, I resumed my prayers.

Needing to urinate, I retreated among the pine trees where the shade was sweeter than the bladder's relief. Sitting down in the shade, leaning against a tree, I glared at the Vision Quest altar baking in the sun. How harsh it seemed! How forbidding! I refused to return to that place of inhumane suffering, couldn't return if I wanted to. Only a fool would risk sunstroke to pray for a Vision.

Whitewolf's warnings about leaving the altar clamored insistently around the edges of my mind. It is dangerous to be outside the altar. The longer I hid in the shade, the less likely I would resume my quest. The Black Tail Deer Spirit, tempted me with shade rather than sex. I realized almost too late that I was being seduced from my altar.

Teeth clenched, I rolled onto my knees, grabbed the tree for balance, hoisted myself up and staggered back to the altar. The Grandfather Sun was pounding me to the ground even before I had lifted my Pipe once again to pray for a Vision. No longer a Hanblecheya, my ordeal had degenerated into a Humble-lechya. I whined, "What fools are we pitiful humans to confront the Grandfather Sun as if to test our power against His." The "I can handle this" boast had been silenced.

The earth turns, indifferent to our struggles. Thus, night once again crept over my parched altar. I was sick. My head hurt. My body felt weak, burned, and pitiful. I grew angry that I had received no Visions or Visitations. The rank unfairness of my plight goaded me. In spite of all my suffering, the Creator was ignoring me. Consumed by anger, Pipe in hand, I confronted the sky.

"Grandfather! This is your grandson, Sings-Alone, down here on a Vision Quest. I am sick. My head is splitting. I am dying, and You aren't doing a damn thing! Are You going to help me or not?"

At that precise moment a shooting star ripped through the air just above my head. I had never heard a meteorite before, but this one sounded like a giant canvass being torn asunder. My initial startle reaction immediately converted to terror. Knees on the ground, I prayed, "Hau! Grandfather. I hear you." Contrition flowed in torrents from my soul.

Properly chastened, I waited alert and thoroughly dehydrated. My mouth was a desert, my tongue a cactus. Hunger was never a problem. My body ached for water.

Later that night a thought shaped itself; a sniggering, cunning, self-serving thought. Soon the dew would fall within my altar. The six inch tall weeds would be covered with luscious, cool, life-preserving water droplets. Everything the Creator put in my altar belonged to me. Nothing else mattered. I craved water. I would soon have water. Beside myself with thirst, I watched as glistening, beckoning beads of God's bounty condensed on the grasses around me.

Pulling a moist blade of grass, I slid it between my lips. Then I pulled and sucked another and another. My tongue demanded more but could not get enough to assuage my thirst. Ripping the grasses from the ground, I sucked right and left. My Sacred Pipe lay abandoned.

A warning sounded in my head, "You can't be destroying your altar by killing the grass!" So, squatting down, I began to suck the leaves without pulling out the plants. Round and round the altar I waddled, crawled, sucked, and licked, tongue searching for each tiny moisture-filled crevasse.

What pleasure! What madness! The more I sucked, the more I craved, so minuscule was the amount until exhausted, I fell, defeated. It was no use! Inside my altar the weeds were torn and trampled into a giant donut shape, mute witness to the night's insanity.

Sunrise! In a few hours Sam would escort me off the hill to the well deserved accolades of my brothers and sisters keeping vigil below. "I could handle" a few more hours.

Without warning, I found myself outside the altar, bundle resting on my right arm, Sacred Pipe clasped in my left hand, propelled down the hill toward the community. I have no memory of what happened between sitting down to wait and descending the hill.

I was angry. After all I had been through, my Hanblecheya should not end this way. A voice at the camp shouted, "He's down! He's down!" Whitewolf, near the lodge, turned to see me stomping across the road. Dropping my Bundle and placing my Pipe on the altar, I crawled into the Sweatlodge. Ripping my bear claw necklace from my neck, I pitched it to Whitewolf and growled, "Put this on my Bundle!"

There were no great Visions to recite nor had my medicine helpers appeared in the night. I was too bitter to recognize the lessons learned in my sun baked altar. Perhaps, I learned more from this Hanblecheya than any of the others. Angry, I announced, "I refuse to ever Vision Quest again."

Pitiful, I added, "I can't handle it."

Mini-Enlightenment

A decade earlier, 1971 – Gainesville, Florida

C harged with excitement, yet spiritually empty, not yet having discovered the Native American path, I searched in all directions for help. It was an era of abundant spiritual guidance. Everything from hallucinogenic drugs, Hindu gurus, yoga practices, and free sex promised salvation and self-actualization. Asceticism suggested a rigorous way to attain a spiritual high. Celibacy promised a straight road to enlightenment by freeing the soul from carnal pursuits and focusing on union with the Gods. Not willing to miss such an opportunity and between marriages, I committed myself to chastity. I could live without sex. As Lord Chesterfield said, "Sex— The pleasure is momentary, the position ridiculous, and the expense damnable." Starting the next morning, my female relationships would be solely platonic. Throughout the night, my resolve strengthened. By morning I was sure of my decision. As the day progressed, the more I professed celibacy, the more I obsessed about sex. By late afternoon, the weight of my decision was crushing my resolve. By nightfall, self-denial overwhelmed me, and Coyote went searching for release. Who knows? I might have become a monk except for my sensually indulgent nature.

I devoured books on personal growth and spiritual development. My doctorate was earned in Humanistic Psychology which at the time was enamored of sensitivity groups, nude encounters, and weekend marathons. Whatever was "in," I wanted to sample. It was a Coyote epoch, a time of exploration and excess.

Somewhere, I stumbled upon a basic truth which was certainly not unique to me. Mystics, healers, yogis, and shamans had practiced it for a thousand years. If you want to fully know or relate to something, be it human, four legged, winged, leafed or stone, stop thinking about it. Our organized minds have a great weakness. We tend to see or perceive what we need to see in order to support our biases. Thus, no two people observing a single event ever remember it the same way.

Simply observing through our senses warps the appearance of what we perceive.

For example, an eagle perched on a barren branch attracts my attention. I immediately determine that it is a bald eagle and estimate its wing spread. I wonder if it is searching for food, and dare muse that it may be a "sign." In the meantime, the eagle lofts itself leaving me with a brain full of chatter. My need to describe and quantify has robbed me of the chance to know the eagle.

The mystic understands that when you relax the body, still the mind, and attend without thinking, you can "know" and "relate" in a clear and intense way. I determined to learn how to become internally quiet and receptive. I took yoga lessons and spent hours staring at a candle flame. At last it dawned on me that I could not muscle myself into quietness. I stopped "doing" anything and "allowed" my mind to become still. In this state of receptivity, I was ready to perceive the world in a radically new way.

We erroneously believe that knowledge comes only through the five senses. Information, however, comes to us through receptors as yet undiscovered by anatomists. For more than two generations parapsychologists have conducted the most meticulous (and boring) experiments studying the Psi Phenomenon; the mind's ability to communicate with other minds, to anticipate events, and to exert force on inanimate objects. In the last twenty years transpersonal psychologists have expanded the study to include the whole realm of Spirit. They have demonstrated what many of us have personally encountered. The mind is not limited by the neurology of the physical body. A quiet, receptive mind is key to perceiving outside and beyond the physical senses.

Soon after I learned how to still my brain, I retreated to the Great Smokies. Although not yet connected to Native American spirituality, I was Cherokee enough to recognize my spiritual home in the mountains. Early one morning I left the cabin and climbed straight up the mountainside where I discovered a small waterfall. At its base a beautiful flower glistened in the moisture and early sun. Something about the scene enticed me. Sitting quietly, I prepared to meet the flower and water without defining either of them. For perhaps the first time in my life I "saw" a flower. I "saw" a waterfall in its singular beauty. I spent the rest of my mountain vacation practicing this new way of relating.

Upon returning home, I heard about the Hindu guru, Baba Muktananda, who had attracted a large following. One of the famous touring gurus of India, reputedly an enlightened Being, he had established an ashram near the University of Florida and would be in Gainesville for a week. His presence in town created a general stir in the more hip quarters of the community. Truth to tell, I was fascinated and wanted to see this Holy Man. At that time I was teaching part-time for the community college, so I arranged an audience for my students with Baba, affectionately called Babaji by his disciples.

In the meantime I read all I could about him and his teaching. His message was clear. If you want to know God, find Him/Her within yourself. Don't look for God in someone else or in a far away place. God dwells within you as you. Yet the ashram was crowded with individuals worshipping Muktananda. When Baba entered the room and assumed his seat on the saffron throne, I opened my heart in quiet receptivity to him. Amazing! I knew this old man. Not yet having the construct, I would later recognize Babaji as a happy Coyote. No matter that he taught his followers to look inward for the Sacred, they insisted on worshipping him, even vying for jars of his bath water! Babaji's eyes danced with mirth. On the one hand he taught Truth, while on the other he passively allowed his disciples their folly. I delighted in his enjoyment of the process.

When the session ended, Muktananda whispered to his translator who pointed at me and said, "Baba wants you to come here." Nonplused, I made my way to the throne and its diminutive occupant. Reaching up and pulling me down into his lap, Babaji gave me a big hug. He spoke to the translator who whispered, "Baba says that you don't need to go to lectures. You already have the Shakti moving within you." I had felt intensely present with him and knew he had met me in that sacred space of knowing. Needless to say my students were wide-eyed. It was quite a rush for me too. My respect for Babaji blossomed as my swollen ego appreciated his acute perception of my great worth.

So when I was invited to participate in a weekend retreat with Baba, I thought, "Why not?" I packed my toothbrush and a change of clothing and headed for the encampment where I was assigned a bunk and given the schedule. The following morning everyone was to arise at 4:30 AM, assemble in the large common room, sit cross-legged on the floor for two hours of meditation, and then have breakfast.

The next morning, along with other groggy participants, I dragged my body to the assembly room and staked out a spot on the floor. Cross-legged, I meditated for fifteen minutes, and then managed to stretch it to thirty. Trying hard to maintain inner quietness, I was dismayed to find my mind filling with chatter and observations. After an hour, all awareness was flooded by acute discomfort. My tortured legs screamed for relief. Whatever its virtues, the Hindu way of meditation was not for me. Staggering to my feet, I fled.

While Hindu meditative postures were uncongenial to me, I believe that the internal mechanisms of meditation and healing are the same in all religions. The task is to find rituals that facilitate them. Unfortunately, my birth religion had failed to connect me with the Sacred in a fulfilling way. Perhaps through over-exposure I had become immune to its power. I required much more than Christian churches could give, so I turned to my racial heritage. In the course of my journey I have also realized that genes are irrelevant. I have known hundreds of non-Indians who found a home on this spiritual path. Some, but certainly not all, Sweatlodge communities welcome Christians, Jews, Muslims, and Bahais, people who are discovering in the simple rituals a way to pray and connect to Grandfather Sky and Grandmother Earth.

Learning to silence the mind is a first step towards a higher spiritual consciousness, but danger still lurks in this process. One can be fooled into believing the mind is out of the way. Then, when you least expect it, the Coyote spirit can plant outrageous notions in your head. Witness the excesses perpetrated by religious mystics sure they were led by the voice of God. Always compare what you are learning in mystic states to what you know is consistent with the highest teachings of your faith. That way you can hold Coyote at bay . . . most of the time.

The Mummy

1973 – My apartment, Gainesville, Florida

In no mood for surprises I stared at the box. It did not belong in my closet, but there it was. An old cardboard box, it was crushed around the edges, and the tape had begun to peel with age. There was an ominous feeling attached to it. I would as soon leave it alone, but could not.

It opened freely. My brain refused to register what I was seeing. The box smelled of age and mold and decay. Cloth remnants, faded to dismal gray, were stuffed inside the carton. Gingerly, as I pushed aside the cloth, my nostrils were assailed by a cloud of dust and old rot. I hated to stick my hand into the mess, probably concealing nesting spiders or mice. Fishing around in the rags I jerked out my hand when it touched something hard. Carefully pulling back the cloths, I first encountered a wee hand, then dark skin stretched over tiny ribs, the desiccated corpse of a little brown baby. Horrified, I closed the box and shoved it way back in the closet.

My life had more than enough complications without finding a corpse in the closet. Recently divorced and spiritually alienated, I was slogging along in the depression of a lost spirit. Late night would find me aimlessly wandering the streets or kneeling before the statue of Mary in the Catholic student parish. Consider an ex-Protestant minister praying to the Blessed Virgin and you will understand how desperately I sought spiritual direction. I did not need a corpse in my closet.

The box obstinately dominated my awareness. Like an elephant in the living room, it would not be ignored.

Finally, I returned to the closet and, with trembling hands, carefully removed the infantile mummy and cradled it in my arms.

Did it really tremble slightly, a tiny movement, an imperceptible twist? Bewildered, I touched its lips with a teaspoon of milk. The mummy smiled and swallowed.

The Medical School sent three doctors, wise men (appropriate since this was mid-December) who examined, in turn, the little corpse. They listened for its heart beat and rocked it side to side, inspecting it with meticulous care. Finally, the spokesman said, "Behold! The mummy lives."

Some people routinely have powerful dreams and keep them in journals. This had not been my experience. I seldom have visionary dreams and had never before experienced a "power dream" but, upon awakening, I knew this one was special.

I telephoned my friend, Colquit, asking him to provide a safe and quiet place for me to process the dream. I did not want him to do anything other than protect my privacy and stay close by.

That evening in the safety of his apartment and friendship, I relived every moment of the dream. An incredible sequence of joy, grief, fear, awe, and love flooded over me. My friend reported that for two hours I laughed, cried, and prayed.

An inner voice was urging me,

"Pay attention! Something very old is about to be born."

The Temple

1973 – A week later.

A large speedboat whisked me through Miami Harbor, past immense cruise ships burdened with overstuffed vacationers returning from the Islands, past pleasure craft displaying lithe, tanned maidens posing provocatively as the wind fluffed and whipped their hair behind them.

Not knowing where I was going or who was taking me, I occupied myself with the scenery. The helmsman navigated wordlessly. A woman, apparently my guide, rode silently at my side. I might have been afraid, but my intuition comforted me. This trip portended some unknown good.

I was having another power dream.

In front of us a mountainous island rose from the sea. It was totally forested, with barely visible structures of various religions tucked away among the trees. I could distinguish a Mosque, a Church, and a Hindu Temple peeking through the trees. Half-way up the hill, leafy shadows mottled a Buddhist shrine. I was baffled.

Our boat circled to the island's left and docked in a small cove. A path snaked up the mountain to a gleaming white temple. Of Grecian style, it boasted tall marble columns surrounding a wide portico. My female guide steered me up the trail and into the temple's gloomy interior. There she directed me down a dim stairway, into a basement.

The light of several candelabra pierced the darkness sufficiently for me to discern row upon row of books, an ancient library. The woman thrust a candle in my hand and said, "Find your own books." Left alone, I explored the library until I discovered the tomes of my ancestors hidden away on a bottom shelf. They were dust-coated, leather-bound volumes, untouched for generations.

How carefully I opened each one. The pages, yellow and brittle with age, were alive with the dreams, visions, hopes, and fears of countless generations of my Grandfathers and Grandmothers. Throughout these pages, ancient voices called to me, sang to me, talked to me. And there, in the flickering light, standing humbly before my ancestral witnesses, I saw myself for the first time.

Several days later, during a meditative trance, a body of clear blue water materialized before me, drawing me like a magnetic force to peer deep into its blueness. A bright golden light startled me. It emerged from the depths, far away but star bright. A voice commanded, "Plunge into the water and in four you will merge with the golden light!"

Of course, this Vision posed many questions. What and where was the blue water? Four what—Years? Days? Months? I had no answers. I somberly concluded that perhaps death impended after a period of four "whatevers," and I would then be absorbed into the Eternal. There was an urgency to the vision, but I had no answers.

The preceding dreams and the vision of the golden light seemed to be connected but unclear in meaning. Perhaps the brown, mummified baby and the ancestral books pointed to my Cherokee heritage, but how were blue water, the golden light and "four" related?

When in doubt about great existential questions, book stores offer the illusion of wisdom. I was enjoying my favorite pastime loitering in our local book emporium when *Rolling Thunder* by Doug Boyd caught my eye. It claimed to be an authentic biography of a living Cherokee/ Shoshone medicine man.

Here was a publication describing American Indian spirituality as a living force. Fascinating! The next day a colleague informed me that Rolling Thunder would be speaking in a couple of weeks to the Southeastern Association of Humanistic Psychology. The meeting at Eagle Mountain, Georgia, an ancient Cherokee holy place, would cover a long weekend.

Up until this point, I had lived in my father's reality. He was a proud Scot with a wee bit of unacknowledged Cherokee blood. My father lived his life for the Church, never wavering in his identity or purpose. I tried vainly to follow him as a clergyman, failed, changed careers, and was currently teaching Psychology courses at the local University. But now, pressed by the dreams, my Vision, and the book, I was determined to meet this living Cherokee medicine man and connect to mother's heritage. I decided to gather some students and go to the Psychology meeting.

I did not see him walk through the crowd to the fire; he seemed to materialize just before the session began. Rolling Thunder wore a white, long-sleeved sport shirt under an Indian vest. His white denim trousers were tucked neatly into high boots. His straw hat sported a wide, beaded headband and a large eagle feather, while from his mouth jutted a corn cob pipe. Though not physically overwhelming, his bearing, his charisma, made him bigger than life.

Standing by a small fire at the base of a natural amphitheater, his daughter-in-law sang some Indian ballads. The wind began to blow smoke in her face choking her voice. We watched, mouths agape, as Rolling Thunder used an eagle feather to change the direction of the breeze. At his back, a large lake rippled lightly in the wind. Eagles circled overhead. We waited impatiently for him to begin. Rolling Thunder finally stood to speak.

The man was witty and wise. The earth wisdom he professed made perfect sense to me. I hung on every word. Several young "warriors" traveling with him drummed and sang, giving us a taste of Native American music. These new experiences resonated deep in my soul even as the drums pounded in my ears.

The morning of the last day, I encountered Rolling Thunder face to face for the first time. He stopped, fixed me with a penetrating look and declared, "You're Indian."

Flushed with embarrassment, I stammered something about my parents having Cherokee blood, all the while kicking myself for denying my heritage.

"No," he insisted, "You are Indian. The old ones say that as long as you have one drop of Indian blood and feel it in your heart, you are Indian."

He continued, "You are miserable, and you are never going to be happy until you know who you are. Come stay with me and I will teach you who you are." I was dumbfounded as he went on, "I want you to come, sit with my young warriors." He always referred to the men of his camp as warriors.

I joined his young men in front of the audience. As Rolling Thunder began his presentation, my students and colleagues were puzzled by my sitting down there, and I, too, felt strange and out of place. Later, he suggested I let my hair grow long and dress "Indian" to get a little notion of how it feels to be "marked" and "different." I think he wanted a visible commitment to changing my life's orientation.

During the following week his words kept echoing in my head, "You are Indian. You are miserable. You will never be happy until you know who you are." He was right on all counts.

I began to make inquiries about jobs that would place me in proximity to Metatantay, Rolling Thunder's camp in Nevada. There was an opening for a psychologist to develop a mental health program for the Colorado River Indian Tribes (CRIT) in Arizona, a half day's drive from Metatantay.

A CRIT representative called to invite me for an interview. Arriving in Phoenix I rented a car and drove to the tribal motel in Parker, Arizona. A message awaited me, "Meet the hiring committee at the Blue Water Marina for lunch." There I found the water to be as beautiful, clear, and blue as in my vision. I scanned its depths without success for a glimpse of the golden light. I had high hopes that the light would soon reveal itself to me. Maybe Coyote would finally leave me alone now that I had learned how to pay attention to the guidance of the Spirits.

Fat Chance.

Moving on Down the Road

1974 – Gainesville, Florida to Parker, Arizona

T he consensus of opinion held that Duncan was certifiably crazy. Colleagues in my private counseling practice could see no reason for me to abandon a lucrative business as a psychologist and professor. Others warned that it was stupid to forsake my support system of family and friends for a tribe of desert Indians. One colleague sneered that because of my long hair and jeans I already looked like an Indian—from a grade B movie. He warned darkly that I would not survive six months on a reservation. Negative advice fell on my head like rain on a duck's back and with the same effect.

Having cried and prayed for meaning in my life, I felt impelled to follow my recent dreams and visions. In addition to two failed marriages, and five children living with their mothers, I exuded a stunted spiritual life. The Creator had offered me a chance to start over and live in balance. Meanwhile, beautiful illusions of becoming a "real" Indian titillated my mind, even as I was tormented by inner doubts that I could survive the Mohave desert.

Regardless of my friends' negativism, the Spirits had granted me unambiguous signs. Somehow, God had noticed me and ordained for me special work. Of course, following close upon such heady moments came experiences to down-size my ego and rebalance my personal universe. Such lessons were rarely easy, especially when the Trickster linked up with my own dark side.

I was a happy camper. The Colorado River Indian Tribes (CRIT) had designated me as their first psychologist. The Tribal hiring committee seemed genuinely interested in having their own counseling center. Mental Health could then become a "Tribal" rather than a U.S. government program, and be housed in the Tribal Office complex, not in the Indian Hospital. I coveted the job, and it was mine.

No chorus of criticism would halt this journey. Coyote was saddled up and ready to ride. Truth to tell, I was the one wearing the saddle.

Light-hearted, I flew back to Gainesville, my life infused with a new sense of direction and purpose. Returning to my roots, proud of being Cherokee, and determined to live "Indian." I would finally be where I belonged. The next weeks skipped by as I closed out my affairs in Florida. At last, with classes finished and final grades submitted, I headed for Arizona. A new Pinto station wagon signaled the commencement of my new life. Every available niche in the wagon was jam-packed with all my worldly possessions.

In my lonely moments, the Trickster would whisper that the critics were right. I would not survive the desert away from my children and friends who cared about me. I couldn't cope in such an alien environment. The Mohaves would ridicule and reject a reborn Cherokee psychologist. Disaster loomed ahead. But for me, there was no turning back. Stifling my fears and ignoring the taunts, I was determined to fulfill my personal odyssey.

After all, the Tribe wanted me. The Tribe hired me. The Tribe would house me. The Tribe would provide all necessary security. I could trust the steadfast and generous nature of "real" Indians who never spoke with "forked" tongues.

The journey west passed without event. By the fourth afternoon I anticipated resting in the waiting arms of the Colorado River Indian Tribes. But as the desert scenery swept by my car window, apprehension gnawed at my gut, as if intuition were warning me that I was about to descend into the most difficult period of my life. Having survived Coyote's lesson of hard knocks, I was about to take his special course in existential despair. Thankfully, I did not know that then, or else I might have turned my vehicle around.

I yearned to embrace the desert without pre-judgement, an impossible chore. The saguaro cacti, like alien sentinels, guarded a desiccated world devoid of living things except for a few birds and an occasional rabbit. Later I would discover a myriad of creatures including rattlesnakes that could stretch themselves across a narrow, two lane road, and I would revel in the profusely blooming desert when the rare rains fell. But my first response yelled that Arizona was no place for me.

The desert mocked me. I shuddered at the parched, hostile environment. How could Indians thrive in such a place? In my mind I thanked the Tribe for providing me with an air-conditioned home. I was determined to follow my dreams and obey the Signs, but thank God for the Mohaves who would support my efforts. It was late afternoon when I arrived at the tribal complex anxious to report and secure keys to my new house.

"Well, hi Dr. Duncan," The tribe's Vice Chairman was all smiles. "Did you have a good trip?"

"It was okay, but I am glad to be here." Truthfully, I was exhausted and hungry. "What I need more than anything is to eat, find my house, take a shower, and get some sleep."

"Good, why don't you do that. Come back tomorrow morning and we can visit then." She politely dismissed me.

"Excuse me, might I have the keys to my living quarters and directions for getting there?"

"Oh, my God," she stammered, "I totally forgot about your house."

For a fleeting moment I thought I saw old Furry, himself, perched on the corner of her desk, huge grin on his face, whispering, "Welcome home."

The long journey and state of exhaustion momentarily befuddled me. This discussion was not making sense. She picked up the phone, dialed it, and conducted a terse conversation. A voice snickered in my ear, teasing me about being helpless with no one to give a damn. Turning to me with a tight smile, the woman apologized, "I am so sorry. We don't have a house available right now. You will have to locate something in town."

I was stunned. They had promised me housing! But I stumbled from the office and, in spite of the late hour, began to search for an apartment. "Something in town" turned out to be nothing. Even the motels were full. I was reduced to finding a camp site.

North of town by the Colorado River a tiny cove, surrounded by stone cliffs, offered haven for the night. The late afternoon sun glared off the pure white sand underfoot. Although this meager refuge was not identified as a camp ground or state park, it sported a bath house. There were no other campers. In this desolate place I pitched a tiny, nylon backpacking tent, my first home in Arizona.

People believe that deserts cool off at night but that is simply not true of the Mohave. The stone mountains absorb the desert heat and radiate its warmth all night long. One hundred degree temperatures at midnight are the summer norm. Inside my tent it must have been one hundred twenty-five degrees. It was not a hospitable place.

On the first night, after trying for several hours to sleep on the blistering sand, I had to answer nature's call. Unzipping the tent, I staggered out into the sweltering darkness searching for the bath house.

A scream ripped the air behind me. Damn near suffering heart failure, I jumped four feet straight up, twisting to face my attacker. Twenty yards away, ears flat and buck teeth shining, a boss burro brayed a second warning to the jennies clustered behind him. Having rendered me helpless with a case of tachycardia, the Burro and his ladies wandered off into the blackness. Meanwhile, in preparation for battle, my bladder had shut down. It took a while to relax sufficiently to finish my business so that I could complete a miserable night in the oven.

The next morning I rose with the sun, offered tobacco, and complained to the Great Spirit, "Why have you sent me to this God-forsaken place?" In less than a day, I had discovered that the land of my Vision was not paradise. It felt more like I had fallen off earth into Hades. While signs in the heavens might be exhilarating, walking the spiritual path could be hell. Like Moses, I had begun an exile in the desert. Unfortunately, the only burning bushes I saw were shimmering from radiated heat.

It was six weeks before the tribe found housing for me deep in the reservation at Poston. It was a community so isolated that it served as a Japanese internment camp during the second World War.

The Invisible Man

1973 – Colorado River Indian Tribes, Parker, Arizona

C oyote knows which of my personal buttons to push, and he teaches me by attacking my vulnerabilities. My ego loves to be fed. From childhood I have enjoyed showing off and being the center of attention.

When I landed on the reservation, I became invisible. The Mohaves had no idea how to relate to a psychologist. Common sense dictated that one should avoid the shrink lest he/she be branded crazy by association. Take it from me, you have never been "invisible" until you have experience being shunned by an entire Indian community. It was especially difficult for me because I wanted everyone to notice and accept me as a special person.

For three days I killed time wandering around the Tribal complex, my only human contact being necessary and official communication with Tribal clerks. The mental health suite remained unfinished, another small item the Tribe had forgotten. The third day I was sitting, alone and lonely, in the lobby of the Tribal Offices. I watched people come and go, yearning to have my presence confirmed by some act of recognition, when suddenly the double doors flew open and an Indian in his mid-thirties strode directly to the information desk. Without warning he crashed to the floor, as if crowned by a club. Clearly, he was having a seizure.

All eyes turned on me. Not a person moved to help. They waited for the new psychologist to act. Moving furniture out of the man's way, I gave him room to thrash about, but he remained immobile. This was not a grand mal seizure. I knelt over him as his breathing grew more and more shallow. It was apparent to me that the man was dying in the main lobby of the Tribal Offices while I, the new shrink, was suppose to save him.

Turning to my audience, I demanded, "Does anyone know this man? Does he have epilepsy?" My voice carried more confidence than I felt.

No one responded. A handful of Mohaves stood watching the new doctor, their faces betraying no emotion at all.

"Call an ambulance," I ordered. No one stirred.

"Call an ambulance now!" Again, no movement.

Turning to the receptionist, I commanded, "You! Call an ambulance right now!" She turned to the switchboard and placed the call.

Bending over the patient, I whispered in his ear, "Don't you dare die on me, you son-of-a-bitch, or I will kill you myself!"

Realizing that something more than a psychological intervention was required, I slid one hand under his skull and the other over his forehead. Taking a deep breath to still my panic and mental static, I focused the Creator's healing energy between my hands. They tingled with the effort. Soon his body relaxed and color flowed back into his face. By the time the ambulance arrived, he was awake. Thank God he lived, albeit forced to wear a neck brace for a while. Had he died, my tenuous acceptance by the tribes might have been destroyed. That horrific episode was my first introduction to alcoholic withdrawal seizures. The man drowned several years later. Dead drunk, he rolled into an irrigation ditch, another victim of the pernicious alcohol abuse that plagues the Indian nations.

This seizure episode signaled to me how much I had to prove to the tribe. Although the tribal officers wanted a mental health program and had hired me, they had no idea what to expect. Truth to tell, most of the people wished I would simply go away. In the meantime, they refused to acknowledge my existence even when the life of one of their own hung in the balance.

It was lonesome trying to be spiritual all by myself. My beautiful dream was fading around the edges. Up to this point my experience of Coyote had been bathed in humor. Being a natural clown, I had enjoyed laughing at my predicaments. But now, I faced the future with grave doubts. Deserted by my internal clown, life devolved into a series of challenges to be endured. Thank God for a few wonderful friends who supported me. Looking back I am puzzled by my internal whining over being lonely and an outsider. What could I have expected, for I was indeed an outsider. I needed to learn some basic lessons about patience, self acceptance, and courage in the face of adversity.

Metatantay

1973, Parker, Arizona where I was Chief Psychologist for the Colorado River Indian Tribes.

R olling Thunder (called RT by friends and family) suggested I visit him before the cold weather swept down through the Sierra Nevada Mountains. Preparing for the trip, I loaded the car with camping equipment, luggage, and offerings of potatoes, apples and other supplies for the camp. An hour before dawn, I left the reservation and headed north on the twelve-hour journey to Carlin, Nevada and Metatantay. Happy for a momentary escape from the Mohave desert, I was ready for my great adventure to begin.

So far, my entry into the Indian world had brought more pain than joy. Consequently, during the entire journey my mood vacillated between anxiety and anticipation. I desperately wanted this trip but shuddered at the possibility of rejection by the Metatantians. I had already discovered on the Colorado River Indian Reservation that being with Indians did not mean being accepted by them. Finally, Carlin loomed on the horizon.

Rolling Thunder sent no directions, but author Doug Boyd had described Metatantay as situated beyond the railroad tracks. His book noted that a hand-printed sign in the yard proclaimed, "No Drugs, No Booze, No Violence." Luckily, only one street crossed the tracks. Directly ahead, a worn frame house slouched against the wind and, peeking from the weeds, a rickety little sign proclaimed its message, "No booze . . . . ."

RT relishes the story that his house was once a railroaders' brothel. It was certainly well placed for those "essential" human services. What irony that the best little whorehouse in Carlin had evolved into a spiritual center. I had no idea what to expect as I parked out front. A couple of young men approached me suspiciously, asking what I wanted. They waited, alert, while I fumbled for Rolling Thunder's letter. When reassured that I had been invited by the boss, they escorted me into the house where RT and several young warriors were drinking dark, boiled coffee.

We chatted innocuously until Rolling Thunder directed, "Go on through that door, and you will find a swing and some chairs under the arbor. Take a seat there. We have chores to do now. Someone will attend to you in a while."

There were two connecting arbors, but one sported a swing, a couple of wooden chairs, and one oversized rocking chair with a battered cushion. The other sheltered only four wooden chairs. There, I later discovered, the young men would drum and sing in the evenings. Obediently, I deposited myself on a bench swing and restlessly waited.

Shades of the reservation. I was bored, cooling my feet again, locked in interminable Indian Time. I had not spent twelve hours driving to Metatantay to stare at the back of a house. Anxiety gave way to irritation. Finally, an older Indian woman appeared, introduced herself as Spotted Fawn, Rolling Thunder's wife, and lowered herself with some difficulty into the oversized rocker. This lady radiated personal power equaled by her substantial physique; five feet tall and two hundred plus pounds.

We discussed my trip and talked about the weather as we appraised each other. Spotted Fawn began asking personal questions like a lawyer taking a deposition, question crowding upon question with little expression of feeling.

"What is your name?"

"C. W. Duncan," I replied.

"Do you have an Indian name?"

"Soquah. It derives from the Cherokee word, soquili, which means horse." I was shamed because I had appropriated the name, not earned it. Maybe she wouldn't ask who bestowed it on me.

"How did you get it?"

My voiced choked and I averted my eyes, "I chose it for myself."

"Huh!" Her grunt expressed her disapproval. "Where are you from?"

"Colorado River Indian Reservation and before that I lived in Florida." I was relieved she did not comment further on my name.

"What do you do on the reservation?" Her voice betrayed no emotional bias. She simply wanted the facts.

"I am a psychologist and I head up the Tribal Mental Health program." I was relieved we were on safe ground.

"What do you want from Rolling Thunder?" Her intensity doubled; this was the bottom line question.

I fumbled for just the right words, "He told me I was Indian and would always be miserable until I found out who I am. He said that he would teach me." As if that was an insufficient or overly selfish reason, I added, "and it is said that he treats alcoholism by traditional and spiritual means. I want to find out about this for my people in Arizona."

Never before or since have I been so quizzed by an Indian. Indian people are generally not intrusive, avoiding personal questions. It is rude to be so personally inquisitive. Years later I realized that this interview was the key to my relationship with Rolling Thunder and Metatantay. It was her job to decide whether I was legitimate and could stay. Apparently, her intuition said I was okay.

Spotted Fawn emerged as a valued friend, one of the truly special people I met out West. Her vigilance was dictated by constant government intrusion into camp life. Each night I was at Metatantay, the police cruised into the compound and questioned those present to "make sure no one was being held against their will." The FBI was infiltrating domestic organizations, particularly Indian groups. AIM (the American Indian Movement) was laced with G Men. Agents in various guises regularly visited Metatantay. They were always recognized in spite of their cleverness.

In Coyote tradition, Rolling Thunder enjoyed playing with the FBI infiltrators. He told about a couple of agents who had visited the previous year. When asked what they wanted, the two men replied, "We are here to find ourselves." After they had settled in, Rolling Thunder informed them that everyone at Metatantay must work. He assigned them the job of transferring two large, reluctant hogs from one pen to another. These porkers were huge, and their pen was knee-deep in muck. The two agents gamely went to work, but being city fellows, they hadn't a clue about how to proceed. Meanwhile, the hogs were in no mood to be hassled. The agents flailed, flipped, and floundered face down in the mud. Rolling Thunder signaled them out of the pen and said, "Now that you have found yourselves, pack up and get out!"

Rolling Thunder had great patience for people who wanted to learn in the Indian way, but he disliked questions. If you worked in Metatantay and paid attention, you would absorb all you needed to know. He would say, "Be quiet, pay attention, and all your questions will be answered in time." Rolling Thunder asserted that he could read your mind and would answer your questions when the time was right. He also insisted that thinking violent or negative thoughts had no place at Metatantay. I felt strange believing anyone could read my thoughts. One morning at sunrise ceremony Rolling Thunder singled out a young warrior and admonished him for unacceptable thinking. The fellow was speechless and shamed to be rebuked so publicly. Of course, Rolling Thunder might have just guessed correctly. Regardless, the effect was dramatic. I sure tried to monitor my own thoughts.

Rolling Thunder taught that the first task in learning the sacred ways was to control one's thinking. He would say, "White people argue that they can't control their minds. That is not true. You can control your mental processes if you want to, and you must do it if you want to walk this path." He was speaking of the intense presence one experiences when the brain is quieted. But more than that, he warned of the potential harm caused by the undisciplined imaginings we project into the universe. The opposite is also true. To use the Powers for good, one must first discipline the mind, for it alone can focus the healing energies which surround us.

Male/female relationships at Metatantay puzzled me. Men and women performed separate roles and functions. Very little interplay between the sexes manifested during the day. Men even ate separately from the women and children. Nightfall brought a curious metamorphosis. That first evening found me resting in the arbor as the young men drummed and sang. The drum resounded through my body until every cell reverberated with its rhythms. Suddenly, a young woman appeared bearing a tray of steaming drinks. After serving the singers, she offered me the last cup and sat down beside me on the swing. The drink exuded a pungent odor, definitely not regular tea or coffee. Embarrassed that I had a drink and she didn't, I offered her my cup.

The young lady shot me a quizzical look, "Women don't drink that."

Missing the point, I asked, "Why not?"

Without hesitation she replied, "We serve that herb tea to our men because it makes them good in bed."

Sexuality was free of the flirting games common to the dominant culture. Spotted Fawn considered it unnatural and a shame for young people to sleep alone, and as camp Mamma, she facilitated sexual communications and contacts. Had I desired to sleep with a certain woman, I would have told Spotted Fawn who would then have inquired if the woman was interested. If the woman was receptive, we would have bedded without a comment or raised eyebrow in the camp. Thus, no one was embarrassed or sexually pressured.

Once a female friend from Florida wrote requesting that I arrange for her and a girl friend to visit Metatantay. Agreeing, I contacted Rolling Thunder, and he assented to their visit. The two young women spent a week at Metatantay. Later, one of them joined her boyfriend at my place in Arizona. This couple, having been separated for more than a month, kept me awake with their sounds of pleasure. The thin wall separating our bedrooms seemed to intensify the racket rather than muffle the passion.

A month later I met Rolling Thunder and Spotted Fawn in Tucson where he was delivering a speech. Spotted Fawn and I explored the area around the hotel. As we rested afterwards, she shyly inquired if the two young women who visited Metatantay were lesbians. She and Rolling Thunder were worried because these girls preferred to sleep together rather than share beds with the young warriors. I assured her that I was certain that at least one of them liked men and told her the story of my sleepless night. Spotted Fawn was visibly relieved.

There was so much to learn about male/female things, about everyday relationships, about the ways of respect in the Indian world. Determined to learn the right way, I watched everything. Each morning the Metatantians would drag out of their beds and congregate in the living-room where Rolling Thunder would be watching the early news on TV. It amazed me that even though there were no windows in the living room, he knew exactly when to take everyone outside for the sunrise ceremony.

At my first dawn in Metatantay I entered the living room, eyes sharp as a hawk to see everything, ears attuned to every nuance. Most of the people were sitting on the couch and chairs. I joined those leaning against the wall, then noticed an overstuffed chair in the corner. Since it was invitingly empty, I walked over and sat down. My rear had no sooner touched the fabric when the whole room was shouting "Get up! Get up!"

"Jesus Christ!" I catapulted upward. "What have I done?"

I whispered to the man next to me, "What's wrong with this chair?"

He replied, "That's a moon chair."

Moon chair etiquette couldn't wait for observational learning. I didn't want to make the same mistake twice. There might be moon tables and moon sinks and moon dogs for all I knew. So, I pursued the line of questioning, "What's a moon chair?"

Condescension dripped from my informant's voice as he instructed this ignorant half-breed in basic behavior, "It's a chair for women in their moon time. You know, when they bleed. Don't ever sit there!"

Thus, I began to fathom the intertwined mores and tenets of the religion and culture. Although the knowledge of moon customs was new and strange, overall I felt I was coming home. Rolling Thunder did not teach me about specific ceremonies, nor did he teach by question and answer. People might spend months at Metatantay and never attend a ceremony other than the Sunrise Prayers around the Sacred Fire. There were no lectures, but every hour brought new learning.

I terminated my first visit with Rolling Thunder after three days. Physically and emotionally exhausted, I returned home to the tribe, but in a more constructive frame of mind and better prepared to do my job. I was welcome to stay longer but overwhelmed with culture shock. The Metatantians did not run me off. I needed to escape and assimilate these experiences. No matter where I went, Metatantay or Mohave, I was still a foreigner in an alien land. But my vision stuck me there, and I would endure until Coyote decided I had learned enough.

Rolling Thunder

1973 – July, Metatantay, Carlin, Nevada

D esert highways can be treacherous. The new ones stretch out in straight lines for miles, but the old ones wind and curve around the dunes and ravines like county roads in West Virginia. Sheer boredom taunts one to take chances. It had been a dull afternoon navigating on such a Mohave road when a subcompact pickup roared by me. Two occupants in open jump seats raised their beverage cans in toast as they blew by. I thought, "Those fools are either drunk, crazy or both."

A few moments later, I slowed behind a couple of cars pulling off the road. Then I saw the tiny pickup lying upside down in the ravine. Two bodies lay motionless 50 feet away from the crumpled wreckage.

Apparently, the truck had hit a sand patch on the curve, lost control, and had flown through the air to the other side of the ravine, smashed head-on into the bank and fell fifty feet backwards to the base of the wadi.

The occupants of other cars were scrambling down the precipitous wall to the wreckage and I followed them. It was tough going, digging in our heels and grabbing hold of any available brush. Carefully we angled our way down. Shaken but safe at the bottom, I took a deep breath and approached the two victims who had been riding unprotected in the back of the pickup. I dreaded the obvious. Both passengers had been broken, mangled, and crushed lifeless in the high speed fall.

Someone found blankets to cover the dead.

By a miracle the man and woman inside the truck cab were alive. We provided primitive first aid until a rescue squad arrived. A number of motorists had stopped and wanted to help. I was grateful for them because it would be very difficult hoisting the survivors up the perpendicular bank. The rescue team quickly stabilized the injured and prepared them for the dash to the hospital.

The pickup's driver was the larger of the two survivors. I grabbed the foot of the stretcher to which he was wrapped and bound. Lifting him, we struggled up the bank. It was back-straining time as I held the rig on my shoulder, dug in my toes for purchase, and grabbed at any available bush with my right hand. It was unthinkable to drop him back down into the ravine. A false move and it could have happened. After much grunting and groaning we deposited him into the waiting ambulance. Once the rescue squad departed with the living, I left, too spent to help retrieve the dead.

Later that night the spirits of the two deceased passengers appeared in my bedroom. When a person dies unexpectedly, the soul is confused, not understanding what has happened and having no clue what to do next. Often the spirit will try to communicate or touch its loved ones and be frustrated by the futility of its effort. It may attach to any available individual open to its presence. Apparently, the two departed souls had returned with me to Parker, Arizona.

I am a lightning rod for spirits. They seem to orient toward me. That dubious talent had gotten me in trouble back during my ministerial days, but I was no longer shocked, afraid, or compromised by "the Other Side." I sensed them hovering close. They needed help in making the transition so I tried to be very concrete in explaining, "I know this is difficult for you and you must be frightened. It was a terrible accident. You died and shed your physical bodies. The other two in the pickup cab survived. At least they were alive when the rescue squad took them. It was unfortunate that your physical life should have ended so abruptly, but now you are on the verge of a new life. Listen carefully. There is nothing I can do for you except give you direction. Be patient for a bit. Watch for Beings of light who will come for you. Go with them and they will carry you across into a new dimension, a new existence. Go now!"

Fatigue saturated my very bones. Sleep overwhelmed my consciousness. When I awoke, the two spirits were gone.

The winding road north of Havasu City reminded me of the accident. I was bored, wanting to get to Metatantay, and pushing the Pinto. There was one spot where the roadway crested sharply and dropped away so fast that the car felt airborne. Hitting that spot I flashed back on the accident and immediately slowed. I wasn't ready to die yet.

Contenting myself with ten miles over the speed limit, I searched the desert's scenery for anything to break monotony. Just when the senses are numbed by sameness, something incredibly beautiful or strange will often appear in the desert landscape. In Nevada, south of Las Vegas, a mirage lake stretches for miles off to the west. It never fails to materialize if the sun is shining. At night, the lights of the city can be seen 20 miles away. On this particular morning Las Vegas was visible many miles before I arrived, the distances abbreviated by clear, dry desert air.

I drove through "sin city" quickly and headed due north, not wanting to lose any time, anxious to see Rolling Thunder again. Suddenly, a neon sign loomed, advertising "The Pussy Cat Ranch (Open 24 Hrs)" and beckoned me. Brothels are legal in parts of Nevada. I had been living a celibate life by necessity rather than choice, and I was lonely for human touch. Maybe I should stop for some fun.

"Yes!" I thought, slowing down, creeping by.

"Yes!" urged Coyote.

There were other "ranches" ahead. I needed to think. This would be an entirely new experience. Lots of men frequent these establishments. Why shouldn't I? But, what does one say at the front door?

Whether from common sense or timidity, I can't say, but I determined that my spiritual quest was more important than a sexual adventure. Celibacy could be borne yet another day.

Arriving at Metatantay late in the afternoon, my whole body was cramped from the drive. In the kitchen I found the coffee pot and relaxed a few moments before setting up my camp. Out behind the house several wickiups had been constructed. These were semi-permanent, domed dwellings constructed somewhat like a sweatlodge, but half above and half below the ground. Inside, a bed was raised a foot off the ground. A wickiup provided safe and fairly comfortable lodging in northern Nevada's summer nights when temperatures might hover in the 30's and 40's.

Across the parking area from the main house and partially hidden by bushes sat a trailer, Rolling Thunder's personal living quarters, off-limits to all but the specially invited. The area behind the main house was overrun by a mammoth collection of castoff furniture, bedsprings, and other salvage. Rolling Thunder would not dispose of anything. "I might have need of that someday," he'd say.

Beyond the junk pile were the pens and sheds for chickens, goats, and pigs. Just behind the wickiups stood a Sweatlodge and the Sunrise Ceremony fire pit. In the lot behind the compound an assortment of decaying cars and trucks was arranged in a straight line. Some ran. Others served as storage. When I found the ground too cold for comfort, Rolling Thunder retrieved a paper sleeping bag from one of the cars. Somewhere he had salvaged a whole car load of these beautifully insulated bags which served my purposes remarkably well. I pitched my tent behind the wickiups, up-wind from the pig pen, which was cleverly constructed of railroad ties stacked like leggos to form hog-proof walls. I noted the unusual use of the ties with appreciation for Indian cleverness.

I had straightened up my stiff back after driving the last tent peg, when Rolling Thunder strode up, puffing his ubiquitous cob pipe, and invited me to a fandango. Achy body be damned, I would not miss this chance to dance even if I didn't know how. Piling into my Pinto, we drove west a couple of hours to a neighboring reservation. The revelries were in full swing by the time we arrived. Indians were dancing around a fire. Elders sat cross-legged under a pavilion, hands moving to and fro in rhythm as they played the bone game.

"Hey you! John Pope!" The voice calling RT by his Anglo name dripped insult and sarcasm. "Why don't you take those White guys out of here. They aren't welcome." An inebriated Indian hurled his challenge from where he slumped against a post. My heart stopped. A nightmare was materializing before me. Astonished dancers froze, awaiting Rolling Thunder's response. Only a fool mocks a man of power.

Rolling Thunder admonished the man, "Be polite."

The drunk retorted, "Get your White boys out of here and get out yourself. The road coming in is the same one leaving. You don't belong here. Go home!"

Rolling Thunder, struggling for self-control, glared at the man and growled, "Didn't your mother teach you any manners?"

The guy persisted, "Go home, John Pope!"

The second insult did it. Rolling Thunder's body tensed and he spoke in a soft, deadly voice, "How about you and me stepping out in the dark to settle this?"

The drunk, sober enough to avoid tempting fate, shut his mouth.

As I had feared, here was manifest evidence that I was resented, an intruder into an alien world. In the meantime, Rolling Thunder had retired to the front seat of a car where he was visiting with the local Chief. They were obviously having a good time. Not knowing what to do with ourselves, RT's young men and I stayed by the fire until the dancers insisted that we join them. Then we danced the night away, enjoying ourselves, appreciative of the hospitality. I had learned a lesson in Indian racism. I had also observed how a medicine man handles a human snake.

Rolling Thunder played himself in the Billy Jack movies, but in the scene where Billy danced with the rattlesnake, RT was Billy's stand-in. In the film, Billy Jack was being trained in Medicine Power by enduring various tests requiring spiritual focus. It was time to dance with the rattlesnake. His supporters had gathered around and Billy Jack stood in a prepared dance arena. A rattler was placed in front of him. RT, playing Billy Jack, began to dance, legs pounding around and over the increasingly agitated snake. The drum throbbed, spiraling upward in speed and intensity. RT danced faster and faster careful not to hurt the snake but pushing it to the limit. The rattler coiled warily at first, then tighter and tighter, the flat brown head, flicking tongue, and slitted eyes tracking RT's every move. Its rattles buzzed a furious warning.

Suddenly, the reptile struck, embedding its fangs so deeply in his leg that it could not break free. Reaching down, Rolling Thunder pulled the snake from his calf. The movie viewer assumed it was a Hollywood stunt. It was not. Rolling Thunder absorbed the snake's poison. Afterwards, the rattlesnake spirit rode him for three days in the Other World.

Most writers honor Rolling Thunder for his supernatural exploits, as if magic best defines the man. Perhaps stories of the paranormal titillate a technological society deprived of spiritual experiences. After reading about him I, too, expected RT to walk on lightning and trembled in awe at the prospect of spending time with him.

That was not the man I came to know. Rolling Thunder certainly had power, but the Rolling Thunder I knew was an Indian man, committed to his people. He struggled with his own demons, buffeted by a relentless Coyote spirit. He was a human being, a two-legged, never labeled a saint. Even in his most heady days I doubt he considered himself holy, but he lived his vision for America's native people. He was a teacher, gathering wounded and lost young Indians from the cities, bringing them to Nevada, and showing them how to live Indian.

I was not the first he had beckoned home. There was Wolf, a Navaho mixed-blood who had been so injured physically and mentally in Viet Nam that he was given up to die. Under RT's care he had made an incredible comeback. Gaining weight and mentally centered, he became a workhorse in the community. There were two other Veterans who were recovering their spirits even though their bodies had not been wounded. You could watch the healing magic work on them.

Buffalo Horse, Spotted Fawn's son by a previous marriage, lived with his bride in a step van near the main house. Several women lived in the main house, but I did not get to know them because the sexes were so segregated. One was Sky, a Chinese woman who would put straight any man invading her space, such as being in the kitchen when it wasn't meal time. Intrusions were not welcome. Even meals were segregated. How strange it seemed to me that the men ate first. It didn't seem fair, but it wasn't a matter of power. Men and women occupied separate spheres and they stayed where they belonged.

Each of the residents was responsible for specific chores. There were animals to be fed and tended and grounds and buildings to be maintained. One of the fellows was a wizard at doctoring the livestock. Those of us who were visitors assisted the others as best we could. I remember helping to hold a very cranky goat who did not want her ulcerous udder to be treated. Two of us had our hands full with her.

Rolling Thunder arranged to lease an adjoining lot which was waist high in weeds. All of the men grabbed sickles and began to wack away, hoping to uncover enough ground for a garden. As we struggled through the tangled growth, we discovered an old motor block hidden deep in the weeds. Laughing, we determined to get rid of it before RT came around or he would insist that it be "saved" along with all the other salvage piled high behind the house. Straining with effort, we had just hoisted the block and were stumbling toward the truck hoping to whisk our cargo away when Rolling Thunder strolled out to check our progress.

Spying our load, his face lit up. "Well, look at that," he said. "Where you boys going with that old motor block?"

"To the dump?" we asked hopefully.

"Naw. Take it over there behind the house. You never know when it might come in handy." He was quite pleased with the find.

While we weren't over-worked, there was always plenty to do, and no one was welcome to be a parasite on the camp. We were honored to be part of RT's dream to build a permanent teaching camp for lost Indians, and we gladly put our hearts and our bodies into it.

On the other side of Carlin lay an alkali flat, a sizable piece of acreage that RT wanted to buy. He dreamed of taking this land, useful for growing nothing but desert sage, and turning it into a self-supporting farm for Metatantay, a place where his city Indians could live and learn. They would raise livestock and vegetables and build a public Indian museum near the highway. Admission to the museum would provide needed cash.

RT had selected the land, had no money to buy it, but fully expected to own it by dreaming the farm into being. RT loaded several of us into my Pinto for a visit to the future Metatantay. Driving well off the road into the field, we parked and clambered out, stretching and getting our bearings. We hiked to the far end of the property, enjoying the exercise, and sharing RT's dream. Looking at the alkali wash, I despaired of anything growing there, but RT had no doubts. It would be a fine place for his people.

From way back in the scrub I spotted a strange car blocking my Pinto's exit. This was no coincidence. Something was wrong. Hurrying back down the trail, we soon made out the familiar Sheriff's seal on the strange car. A deputy was sitting in the passenger's side of my Pinto. Rushing up to the driver's side, I asked him what he wanted. The contents of my glove compartment lay rifled in his lap.

He offered a lame explanation, "Well, I found your car here and thought there might be a dead body in it or somethin'." I recognized him as one of the cops who had harassed us in RT's driveway the night before.

Getting out of my car, he drew himself up to his full height. Patting his pistol, he warned that he was armed and prepared to deal with weird cults and miscreants. I guessed that he meant us. It wasn't the first time that I had heard Indians referred to as a cult. Strange! Obviously, being Indian in itself was cause for suspicion. Making the point that he was boss in those parts, he gave us a warning glare, jumped into his squad car and drove off.

Rolling Thunder not only fought for Indian justice, he insisted on impeccable behavior from Metatantians. Several of the guys planned a sweatlodge ceremony but needed firewood to heat the stones. A tree had fallen in the pasture on a nearby ranch. It would provide enough wood for several sweats.

It seemed like trespassing to me, but I lamely trusted his young men to know what they were doing. Jumping into the truck and my Pinto, we drove alongside the railroad bed for nearly a mile. Finally reaching a spot where we could cross the tracks, even though it was not a legal crossing, we bumped over to the other side and down a dirt path through a broken gate into a pasture. I wasn't sure that my Pinto was equal to such rough treatment, and I was equally worried about being on someone else's turf. I furtively looked around to see if we were being watched.

Off to one side of the pasture lay a pile of limbs and branches which we heaped onto the truck. Fully loaded, we headed back toward Metatantay. As we drove through the gate, a cowboy sat motionless on his horse, half-hidden by the trees. My face burned with embarrassment, feeling I had been caught red-handed, but the others either failed to notice or did not care.

Later that afternoon with the wood unloaded, we rested in the shade. My reverie was interrupted by the slow clomp-clomp of a horse's hooves. From my vantage point on the ground there appeared before me a giant horse being ridden by a classic John Wayne character in jeans, a long sleeved western shirt, and a ten gallon hat. A cigarette dangled from his lips. A colt '45 snuggled at his hip; a cased rifle hung from his saddle. His eyes glinted like cold steel.

Fixing us with his frigid gaze, he demanded, "Where is Rolling Thunder?"

"He's not here. He's on the road," we replied with one voice.

"Where is Buffalo Horse?" His voice was flat.

"Here I am. What can I do for you?" Buffalo stepped forward.

"You boys took that brushpile off my property today," the cowboy spoke evenly.

'Dammit, I knew we had no business on that ranch,' I said to myself.

"That's OK," the cowpoke continued. "I was going to burn it anyway. But you should have asked first."

We breathed a collective sigh.

He hadn't finished, "The other day you stole a bunch of railroad ties that I intend to use to build me a bridge. I want them returned before sundown." The pig pen! I made an instant connection to the leggo walls of hog haven. Having spoken his piece, he wheeled the horse around and sauntered slowly out of the compound. I could have sworn the horse emulated the stiff-legged walk of an old western gun slinger.

We returned the railroad ties, and the pigs retired to less commodious accommodations.

When Rolling Thunder discovered what had happened, he was furious. "I have told you boys to get along with these ranchers. I had assumed you had asked for those railroad ties. I don't want that man having to come here and reclaim his property ever again. Never!" Even though I had not participated in the theft of the railroad ties, it made no difference. I felt guilty and was reminded again that an Indian lives in a hostile world. You best not cause problems for yourself and don't leave the Trickster room to make trouble for you.

Coyote enjoyed a good home at Metatantay. There were always young fools available to victimize. Rolling Thunder, having a great sense of humor and loving to tease, was a willing partner for Coyote.

"Rolling Thunder," I asked, "Is it OK to have more than one wife at the same time?"

"You can have as many wives as you can support but," he continued, checking to make sure that Spotted Fawn and the women were listening, "the important thing is to never stop with only two. Either have just one wife or three. Two wives can always turn against you. Then you are alone. But, no three women can agree on anything, so with three wives there will always be one to take care of you."

I think he believed the teaching, but RT was mostly goading the women. When I asked him about it years later with my wife present, he chuckled that having multiple wives was her choice, not mine.

I felt safe but still a fish out of water at Metatantay where my only responsibilities consisted of keeping quiet and paying attention. Rolling Thunder laughed, "We think white people are rather retarded. The only way they learn is by asking questions and endless talking. Indians learn by keeping their eyes open. Everything you need to know at Metatantay can be learned by observation."

Teachers Everywhere

1973 – Colorado River Indian Tribes, Parker, Arizona

I n time, the people on the Colorado River Indian Reservation began to accept me. Amused by this Easterner who called himself a Cherokee, they needled me with their insinuations that every Anglo passing through the reservation had a Cherokee Princess Grandmother, adding that Cherokees sure sported a lot of royalty. The people treated me no worse or better than they did each other with their laughing and teasing.

Once they trusted me and knew of my spiritual interests, friends pointed me towards various medicine articles . . . hawk feathers . . . pelts . . . beads . . . herbs. A young Chemehuevi man gifted me a perfect, golden eagle tail feather, told me how to pray with it and use it for protection. He promised that the feather would take care of me. Years later that feather hung in my hair during Vision Quests. It remains a special helper.*

Having learned from Rolling Thunder to be quiet and listen, I absorbed teachings from many sources. Eagle feathers are powerful tools for healing and protection. They focus and empower the intention of the healer. Sage rolled into a ball and lit produces a smoke that drives away evil forces. Likewise, flat cedar thrown onto live coals will clean the air and call forth the Creator's good Spirits. Ocean salt sprinkled around the room with a spoonful in each corner is also an excellent purifier.

Like a sponge, I soaked up information. The tribal archeologist cautioned me about going into certain desert places alone. He warned that these localities were filled with Evil Spirits under control of Tribal brujos. He had made that mistake and nearly died before being rescued by a Mohave witch who took pity on him.

I had bought an Indian ring in Florida. Fashioned simply of silver and turquoise, the stone had a peculiar milky streak through it. One evening a friend and I were eating in the local restaurant when an

Indian shoved through the front door. He was on crutches and made his way directly to the counter on the opposite side of the room. We noted him because of his difficulty in walking. Abruptly, he turned from the counter and hobbled over to our table . Without introduction he said, "That is a very important ring you are wearing. Don't let it get away from you. The creamy streak through it is your pathway between the worlds." With that, he turned back toward the counter. I called out, "Wait a minute. Come join us." He returned to our table for an evening of food and conversation, but spoke no more of the ring. Later that evening he invited us to his home way down in the reservation. We drank coffee and talked on into the night. His was a lovely, generous spirit. I will never forget that evening, and I still wear the ring.

In most cases, the local people exhibited great patience with me. Occasionally I would be derisively labeled, "Super Indian," but by and large they accepted me as a needy mixed-blood who was determined to find a spiritual home. Some of my later stories would leave one thinking that the desert provided only lonely, dangerous and embarrassing experiences. Not true. Many of the tribe's people befriended me. Some remain friends to this day. After my initial disaster in the desert, not a day on the reservation passed without my feeling privileged to be there, nor did a day go by without my feeling like a stranger in a strange land. Coyote never let me off the hook. To walk this sacred road, I had to start at zero and be torn down so completely that there was no way to go but up. Not that the people wanted me to suffer. The truth was I was an outsider. But the alienation festered in my heart, not theirs. I was honored by the people's trust and enriched by their good humor and spirituality. As with my visits to Metatantay, it was not my time for ceremony or ritual, but to get straight who I was and wasn't. Maybe it was synchronicity. If I felt alienated, a foreigner on the reservation, it dawned on me how much more that Indian people, who belong on this continent, have been made to feel alien and unwelcome in their own land. Thanks to the Furry One, I was beginning to understand.

Arriving in Arizona, I had expected to be welcomed as a mixed-blood Cherokee wanting to find himself. The whole notion amused my hosts. Receiving me as a person, another human being, albeit a bizarre one at times, they cared not a whit about my blood quantum or my quest. On the other hand, I had chosen them because they were Indians, a connection to my roots. Wanting to be just like the people,

I immediately discovered that Indianess could not be donned like a coat. I could only be myself and evolve into whatever I would become. Besides, there was no typical *them* to emulate. They were human beings who just happened to be Mohave, Chemehuevi, Navaho, or Hopi.

* I have a federal permit for eagle parts. I mention that because the government rightfully cracked down on the trafficking in eagles. An endangered species, they were hunted by Indian and Anglo opportunists looking to make a fast buck.

The Mystic Desert

1974 – Colorado River Indian Tribes, Parker, Arizona

The desert in Arizona remained a source of fearful fascination. The mountains daunted me. Back East, the Smoky and Blue Ridge Mountains beckon one to explore their peaks and valleys. They are mysterious, soft and inviting. The stone mountains around the reservation dare you to invade them. Life, while abundant on those ridges, wears a desert camouflage. Occasionally one stumbles into a hidden canyon flourishing with trees and shrubs. I found a few such places, but usually perception is dulled by the monotony of sand and stone.

Moon Mountain was named for it's large deposit of crystals that reflected moonlight. Taking a tobacco offering for the Spirits, I drove as close as possible to the mountain and searched until I located a path leading upwards. What a thrill to walk those ageless trails. Well up the trail it dawned on me that the locals stayed off the mountain. The paths were old and did not show the wear associated with recent human use. There was no litter of any kind. I found ancient petroglyphs and the crystal deposits. I wondered why the Mohaves avoided such an awesome mountain.

When Colquit, my rock climbing friend, arrived to spend a few months, I took him to Moon Mountain. Having been there several times, I knew the paths well. The day promised adventure. It kept its word.

We spent hours exploring the mountain, investigating side paths, and delighting in the forbidden beauty of the place. Late in the afternoon we began to retrace our journey back to the desert floor. Far below us we could barely discern my motorcycle half hidden under a scrawny mesquite tree. Colquit suggested that instead of following the path, we scramble down the side of the mountain. I demurred. Having a phobia of heights and not comfortable even on a step ladder, I wanted no surprises. I knew the regular path could be descended by anyone. What might await us down the mountain side was a complete unknown.

"Colquit," I insisted, "There is no way I'll leave the path. There are no guarantees that we can get down without rock climbing, and I won't do that."

When he demanded that we take the short cut, I told him to go on alone. I would go back the way I came. Colquit argued, reasoned, and finally prevailed. He assured me that it would be a simple trip. So, with misgivings I followed him, slipping and sliding, down the west side of Moon Mountain where we found ourselves in a hidden canyon lush with plant life. Following the canyon to its opening, we faced another scramble downward which led to my undoing.

The trail ended at the top of a dry waterfall. With precipitous sides cutting off alternate routes, our only choice was to climb down the rock face of the water fall. Thank God that there was no water flowing in the creek.

I froze. In the meantime, Colquit climbed down the bare rock with no trouble at all. Like a huge spider he worked his way back up to where I stood in mute rebellion. Finally he coaxed me over the edge by promising to guide my feet to each required foothold. I was well out on the rock face, trying desperately not to hug the cliff but to keep space between my body and the stone surface. I carefully followed his directions until I ran out of hand holds. Then I was simply stuck, somewhere between heaven and earth, on some damned forsaken rock. Thanks to my dear friend, I hung there, cursing the day I had ever met him. I questioned his family tree, his genetic background, the species of his mother. I cursed the mountain. With horror I felt my sweaty fingertips slide a fraction of an inch, then another.

"Colquit," I screamed, "I'm coming off this son-of-a-bitch. I'm going to fall!"

"Well, alright," he said from below. "Go ahead and push back from the cliff and fall straight down."

With a silent, desperate prayer, I kicked back and fell.

Twelve inches.

I had been too petrified to look down, and my "friend" had let me think I was high up on the rock instead of almost on the ground.

The fool, his friend, and one grinning Coyote straddled the motorcycle and headed back for Poston.

It hadn't occurred to me that we were intruding into sacred space, that there were reasons those trails weren't used. How typical of an outsider to explore Indian places without asking permission. I knew that the mountain was sacred. Naively, I assumed I would be welcomed if tobacco were offered first. If Mohaves avoided Moon Mountain, a half-breed acculturated Cherokee should have taken the hint and stayed away. I hope that the people forgave my lapse of sensitivity and respect. Obviously, the Spirits of Moon Mountain had pity on me for they did not strike me down.

Evenings in the desert carried a chorus of coyote song. I loved the nightly chorale. My yard backed up to the desert's edge where the coyotes sang at my rear windows.

One night, carrying my eagle feather for protection, I walked out into the desert to pray under the stars. Clay roadways ran along the irrigation ditches which brought water to the nearby farms. By one of those ditches I stopped, raised my eagle feather, and began to speak. I heard a sniff off to my left. I stopped to listen. Then came a sniff on the other side, inquisitive little sniffs all around. I was either surrounded by coyotes, or I had stumbled into a Spirit gathering. Using my feather as a shield, I began to back down the road until I could retreat with some dignity to my house. Afterwards I avoided walking in the desert at night. I would, however, ride my motorcycle deep into the desert believing I could outrun any hostile denizens of the dark.

In spite of the exotic flora and fauna I never felt at home in the desert. Being an easterner, my eyes yearned for green. They were satiated by brown. Regardless, no one had run me off yet. The naysayers back home were wrong. I would stay so long as the Creator wanted me there.

That Lecherous Coyote!

A Traditional Hopi Tale

C oyote was a good hunter. He usually provided plenty of meat for his woman and their young ones. She had only one complaint about him. He chased every female he could find. Not that he lacked sex; she was always available. He wanted new sex, new conquests. Fresh flesh raised his machismo to full power.

One afternoon as he, his woman, and their cubs were exploring, they became thirsty. Searching near the base of a cliff, they spotted a bubbling spring. A family of spiders inhabited the nearby rocks.

As Coyote's family bent down to drink, they were surprised to discover little spider children splashing and playing in the water. Rather than disturb them, the coyotes watched with enjoyment and waited.

A voice commanded, "All of you, out of the water now. Our visitors are thirsty and want to drink." The little creatures scrambled out of the water, and the voice continued, "Good afternoon Coyote family. You must be thirsty on such a hot day. Go ahead and drink all you want."

Coyote looked around trying to locate the voice. Finally he saw a mama spider dangling from a web over their heads. She urged them to drink even more. In a few moments the spider husband joined his wife in visiting with the Coyote family. The adults complimented each others' children and enjoyed the cool shade and company until late afternoon.

When time came to return home, Coyote invited the spiders to come for dinner in a couple of days at his den. The spiders agreed.

Because they are so small, the spiders started a day early and began their trek across the desert to Coyote's place, a slow trip for this little family. The sun set before they had completed their journey, and the spiders spent the night in a warm rock crevice. Starting early the next morning, they reached Coyote's place around noon.

The two families enjoyed visiting and shared a sumptuous feast of rabbit and field mice.

By late afternoon, the spiders prepared to return home, but Coyote urged them to stay until morning. Appreciating the offer, the spiders located a large crack in the rock and bedded there for the night. The next morning the spiders profusely thanked their hosts for all their hospitality and insisted that the coyotes dine with them in three days.

Even though the coyotes accepted, they weren't too happy about it. "It will be a poor feast that spiders could provide for us," grumbled Coyote. His wife and the cubs all agreed, but politeness dictated that they go.

So, early on the third day, the coyotes trotted across the desert to the spider home by the cliff. A fine meal was spread before them, although perhaps a rather strange meal for coyotes. On the table were cobweb bowls of gruel speckled with dead flies.

Although coyotes loved gruel, they had never tasted decomposed flies. They paused while the spiders dug in with gusto. Finally, Coyote took a bite and his family followed suit. "Hmm, that was pretty good!" Each tiny bite mixed with their saliva magically expanded into a big mouthful. Thus, satiated, the coyotes applauded the wonderful feast.

Afterwards, everyone flopped down for a nice nap. When they awoke, Mother spider said, "Don't go home yet. I want to entertain the kids." She led the children to a special place at the cliff's base where she pushed four sticks into the ground. Then, spinning a web round and round the sticks, she created a large basket.

Mother spider invited the Coyote pups to watch the game she played with her babies. The pups could take the second turn. First, she placed her babies in the basket. She pulled a silken strand from her vulva and attached it to the basket. With the basket securely tied to her body, she climbed the cliff. Reaching the cliff top, she warned the babies to hold tight and she pushed the basket over the edge, letting it down by a thread which she rapidly span from her vulva.

The children squealed and laughed, begging her at first to let it go faster, then crying that it went too fast. Finally they reached the bottom.

Then, it was the pups' turn. "Don't be afraid," laughed the spider babies, "there's nothing to it, and it's lots of fun."

Mamma spider lowered herself to the ground and herded the pups into the basket. She warned them, "Don't wiggle around too much, and don't look up at me. You might see something staring back at you which could be upsetting, so keep your eyes turned down." She obviously did not want them looking at her private parts as she dragged the basket up the cliff. Once again, reaching the top, she let the basket of pups descend in a fun-filled, controlled fall. The children of both families loved the game and repeated the trip over and over again.

Too soon it was time for the coyotes to leave. The spiders packed them some traveling food, and the coyotes trotted home quietly in the early darkness.

Arriving home, old man Coyote fantasized about Spider Woman. Having never had sex with a spider, he began to scheme how he could seduce her. If he could get Spider Woman to hoist him up the cliff in her basket, he would be able to peer under her skirt. Then, alone at the top of the cliff, he would take her.

After a few days Coyote's woman told him that they were low on meat and he would need to go hunting. Coyote awoke early the next morning, but instead of hunting, he slipped away to the spider spring by the cliff.

Coyote squandered hours gossiping with his spider friends. Anxiously, Spider Man noticed how coyote kept brushing his tail against Spider Woman. Spider Man worried about the intense way Coyote's eyes tracked his wife's every movement.

After a while, Coyote said that he should start hunting, and he believed that plenty of game grazed near the cliff's top. Coyote wondered aloud, "Spider Woman, do you think that you could carry me up the cliff the way you hoisted the children? If I kill game up there, I will share half of it with you."

Spider Woman concurred, but her husband whispered for her to beware, "I wish you hadn't agreed. I think he may try something. I don't like the way he looks at you and lets his tail brush against you."

Coyote was already making his way to the cliff in a lather to sneak a peak under her skirt. Spider Woman, forewarned by her husband, arrived at the site and began to spin a basket. Upon finishing, she warned Coyote, "Close your eyes tightly as we ascend. If you look up you will create real trouble for yourself. Keep your eyes shut!"

Coyote readily agreed, but as soon as Spider Woman began to hoist him upward, Coyote peeked out of the basket with one eye. Sure enough her vulva showed clearly. Coyote's tongue was drooling and his eyes fairly bulged. He wanted to have Spider Woman in the worst way! He could hardly wait until they were on the cliff top where he would seize her and copulate with her.

Coyote shifted onto his knees in order to stare directly under her skirt. With an enormous erection demanding satisfaction, he could not resist fondling himself. Spider Woman warned him, "Hold still down there. I know what you are doing. I warned you to keep your eyes closed but you are being indecent with me. Now hold still, or you may cause the basket to fall."

Coyote tried to stop moving. He squeezed his penis tightly, while his eyes stayed fixed on her private parts. Finally, overwhelmed with lust, he jumped straight up toward the object of his fascination. The sudden movement wrenched the basket away from Spider Woman and sent it hurtling down the cliff.

Coyote was so caught up in his sexual fantasies that he exploded in orgasm just as the basket slammed into the ground. Thus, Coyote climaxed and died at one and the same moment.

Spider Woman looked down the cliff face at the dead coyote, no pity in her heart, "You dirty old coyote. You got just what you deserved."

Horns of a Dilemma

1973 – Life on the reservation

readfully lonely, I missed dating. Once I was free of the ministry, women had become the objects of my pursuit and pleasure. I was disappointed when the tribal planner, a white man, confided that Mohaves resented outsiders dating their women. One summer afternoon, lonely and horny, I visited the bar in town, reputably a place to pick up non-Indian women. Not a particularly shrewd move.

Seldom frequenting bars, I felt out of place pushing open the doors of The Pit Stop. Taking a moment to let my eyes adjust to the darkness, I made my way to the bar. Grabbing a stool, I perched there, anxiously awaiting the bartender to take my order. Holding my beer, I scanned the room to discover that the only other patron was a lone woman sitting across from me. She smiled hopefully. I smiled back, took a sip of beer, and rehearsed my next move. I had never done this before, but it seemed simple enough. I would buy the lady a beer and see what happened next.

Suddenly the "voice" of common sense stopped me dead in my tracks. The words filled my cranium, "You fool. You have never picked up a woman in a bar. You will not begin today!" Now I was torn between conflicting demands. Here was a woman wanting company. My macho self insisted that I go ahead. "Don't be a fool. She's all yours," Coyote hissed. But my own inner voice dictated that I cut my losses and run. Dismayed, I gulped down my beer, smiled a brief goodby, and fled the bar. So much for picking up women in the local drinking hole.

This left me at square one in finding female company.

Arizona Western College had contracted with me to teach a communication skills class in the city of Parker. I liked colleges and college coeds. A few class members were non-Indians, among which was Sarah, a young nurse from the Tribal hospital. It turned out that she was an Osage breed but, at least, she wasn't local. Besides, she was very attractive. I noticed her long, straight blond hair, tight jeans, and blue eyes the first time she walked across the room. My ego was flattered by the way she hung on my every word, asked intelligent questions. As part of the class, she composed a perceptive essay describing herself as lonely and between relationships. Bingo! I would not miss such an opportunity.

That weekend we laughed our way through supper, both of us enjoying the break from our enforced loneliness. She was lovely and desirable, so I enticed her onto my motorcycle, and took her into the desert to watch the stars. Without humidity's filter and the bleaching effect of city lights, the desert sky was incredible. The stars appeared to be within arms' reach. We could see a hundred times as many stars with our naked eyes in the desert as we used to see in the city. They were extremely bright. How romantic to fly free on a motorcycle beneath the desert canopy!

The night passed in play. Laughter led to passion. We shared our dreams and goals. Sarah understood that the remainder of my life was dedicated to learning and living "Indian." Life in the arid desert had begun to blossom. Soon thereafter, Sarah moved into my home. Two lost souls locked on to each other.

My little community, Poston, possessed an infamous history. One of the Japanese internment camps had been situated there. My place originally had served the internment camp commandant. Additional houses nearby had sheltered various camp personnel. In one of those houses the tribe's social services agency managed a foster home for children. We all coexisted happily.

My household began to expand. Sarah and I were soon joined by Dana, a Creek Indian hired to work with young people in the alcoholism program. Then his girlfriend appeared from back East. Next arrived another alcoholism counselor who was regularly visited by his girlfriend. Our happy little cottage was further occupied periodically by visitors from Florida. I was landlord to a rollicking, lusty establishment.

Kids from the tribal foster home swarmed over the community like a pack of puppies investigating everything and full of childish mischief. One evening my house was rocking with their play. A sharp warning in my head sent me pell mell down the hall just as a curious eight-year-old lifted my loaded revolver from the dresser drawer. Panicked, I snatched the gun from his hand and shooed the kids from the house.

My good-time home had nearly become the site of unimaginable tragedy. I was lucky.

That marked the beginning of the end of the party.

Our life on the reservation took a sudden turn when the coordinator of tribal Social Services appeared in my office. After a few pleasantries, she remarked, "We see a lot of cars over at your place."

"Yes," I responded, pleased that she had noticed my generosity and hospitality, virtues among Indian people.

"We notice that one of the cars belongs to that nurse up at the hospital." She arched her eyebrows.

"Un huh," I agreed. I knew I was in trouble and the noose was tightening.

"Well, what we want to know is, do you believe in this new morality?" Her eyebrows lowered menacingly.

"What do you mean?" I asked cautiously.

"You and that nurse. Are you living together not married? We don't agree with that kind of thing." Her eyebrows rested on her glasses now as she leaned forward like some great Mamma preparing to kick ass.

Neither Sarah nor I wanted to live alone in such a stark, lonely environment and besides, we were having fun. Rather than cause a scandal, we got married. Our union solved one problem but exposed another. Soon after our marriage, Sarah confessed that while she had made some Indian friends, she disliked reservation life and wanted to move back East.

Dana, traumatized by the rigors and violence of reservation life, returned to Florida. The alcoholism counselor married his sweetheart, and they found their own home. Friends from back East stopped visiting. The house grew lonely with just the two of us.

Sarah and I determined to put space between us and the prying eyes of Social Services. Soon we moved off the reservation to an apartment in Parker. There our life together degenerated into sullen mutuality. She hated being there while I had moved half way across the country following my dream.

Truth to tell, having spent a couple of years in the desert, I too was growing lonesome for the East Coast. When Sarah was transferred by the Public Health Service to the National Institutes Of Health in Maryland, I was ready to go with her. After the endless brown of the desert, the Maryland forests were a balm for both my eyes and my soul.

I rejoined academia as Assistant Professor of Clinical Psychology for Antioch University, Columbia, Maryland campus. Coyote must have been satisfied that I had learned my lessons well and could go home. My desert sojourn was finished.

Transformations

1976 – Whitewolf's place, rural Maryland

I met my spiritual teacher, Whitewolf, after moving back to Maryland. Missing Indian people, I feared losing my direction once again. Someone mentioned an Indian store in Ellicott City, Maryland, a once prosperous factory town on the banks of the Patapsco River. Ravaged by time and floods, the factory had crumbled into a rusted skeleton. The usual commerce of Main Street had given way to a chaotic assortment of antique stores, specialty shops and cafes.

In this unlikely setting I discovered 'Whitewolf's Trading Post' a shop tucked in behind a jewelry store. Occupying one modest room, it contained several showcases filled with beadwork, buckles, bolos, and Pipes. The wall displayed lances and original art. Behind the counter, a heavy-set man barely acknowledged my presence. His faded tee shirt peeked out beneath a leather vest. His jeans, tightly cinched below his belly, clung desperately to his hips, while his head sported a vintage black Stetson with woven band and an eagle feather. Whitewolf's presence dominated the room.

Two Indians meeting are a bit like strange dogs sniffing each other. I questioned him about some of the art work. He asked where I came from as I was wearing southwest Indian jewelry. Indians are not paranoid. Just careful. Bitter experience has taught us about fake teachers as well as eager seekers with hidden agendas. Too many people have attended ceremony a few times, then publicized themselves as Native American shamans. Their pirated ceremonies are extremely offensive to us. Imagine a Catholic response to someone pretending to be a priest and offering his version of the Mass. So it took a while for Whitewolf to gamble that I had no ulterior motives. His acceptance depended on intuition, common acquaintances (everyone knows someone in the Indian world), my work on the reservation, and my patience in getting acquainted with him.

Being too eager would have been a short cut to rejection. After several visits at the store, he invited me to ceremony at "Whitewolf's Paradise." The name was an inside joke, a parody of "Crow Dog's Paradise," the South Dakota camp of a well known medicine man, Leonard Crow Dog.

The week before the ceremony crept by, but Saturday morning arrived right on time. I was happy and excited as I pointed my car toward Baltimore. Following his directions, I drove the winding road over the ancient Patapsco River bridge, up the nearly vertical Quaker Hill, and bounced around corners. The road slowed to one lane over the creek. I finally arrived at his driveway. Taking a deep breath, I turned right.

This final quarter mile was a trip in itself and not to be believed. In and out of ruts, tipping wildly in both directions, I crept up the driveway. To the left, a thicket of bushes and trees rose straight up an impressive hill. To the right, what had possibly been a planted field at one time was now an impenetrable patch of weeds and briars. Ahead I saw an ancient farm house with the skeleton of a two-story addition tacked on the side. A bunch of cars clogged the drive near the house. Young men moved purposefully back and forth. As my car emerged into the parking area, I saw the object of their attention standing in an open lawn to the right. The Sweatlodge, a low, igloo-shaped structure covered with blankets and tarps, faced a bonfire being tended by three young men. Just beyond the lodge, a narrow creek splashed noisily over rocks, made a sharp turn, and opened into a perfect swimming hole. I later discovered that a family of water snakes shared this pool with sweaty Indians after Inipi. The snakes would shelter under the opposite bank until the two-leggeds left.

Pausing in the driveway, I called to one of the men, "Where can I find Whitewolf?"

Nodding his head toward the house, he replied, "In there."

Finding an empty spot, I parked my car, and emerged stiffly into a scene of jumbled chaos. To my left, old bed springs, pieces of metal and assorted junk lay scrambled with trash in a heap. In front of me an overgrown path hinted at what was once a single track road leading toward the rear of the camp. A decaying barn tilted precariously toward the creek. Behind me a steep, clay bank led up from the parking area toward the house. An assortment of boards bridged mud patches from previous rains and led to a porch which had suffered too many feet, too much rain, and too little maintenance. One board in front of the door was mostly rotted away. It would remain so for the next seven years I would walk across it. The door yawned open. Tentatively sticking my head inside, I discovered Whitewolf working behind a card table piled high with leather scraps. A couple of men smoking cigarettes were lounging on the furniture. Craft materials, artifacts, coats, blankets, and books filled every nook and cranny.

Whitewolf spotted me, "Hau, come on in."

"Thanks."

"I see you found us. Have any trouble?"

"No," I responded. "Your directions were right on."

"There's coffee in there," he said pointing toward the kitchen.

I found the pot, uncovered a spare cup, and served myself.

Having said, "Hello," Whitewolf returned to his previous conversation as he focused his attention on the work he was doing. He earned his entire livelihood as an artisan supplying Indian crafts and buckskin clothing to connoisseurs from coast to coast.

No one paid much attention to me. Whitewolf later confided that he reckoned I was another one of the "Whiffos" who appear, attend a sweat or two, discover that the religion is hard and unglamorous, and disappear into the night.

Not me! Once I had found Whitewolf, I would not leave unless the Spirits sent me away. I had been on my quest for several years, following my dreams from Florida to Arizona and now to Maryland. From Rolling Thunder I learned the ways of respect, but he was not my spiritual teacher. I owe him a debt of gratitude for he was the first to set my feet on the Red Road. But Whitewolf was special to me. He was real. His genuineness and sincerity impressed me from the beginning. He had no gimmicks and he promised nothing, least of all instant shamanism. I had learned from Rolling Thunder that ceremonies could not be bought. Healings were not for sale. The religion could not be commercialized. An authentic teacher is not in the "business" of teaching. I was pleased to find that Whitewolf felt the same.

An hour or so after I arrived, the stones were ready, glowing hot. A general commotion ensued, and I followed Whitewolf and the other men outside to the fire. Sacred Bundles were opened and Indian Pipes joined, stem to bowl, as the men knelt to prayerfully load them with tobacco. Sacred Pipes filled and placed on the Buffalo Skull Altar, the men stripped, wrapped towels around their waists, and paused by the lodge door as Whitewolf completed his preparations.

I was invited to participate by helping outside the lodge. Whitewolf usually required "first timers" to attend the door as preparation for their first Sweat. The door keeper fishes the hot stones from the fire and carries them on a pitch fork to the lodge. He passes in the sacred herbs and the water as requested. Most importantly, he listens carefully for the call, "Mitakuye Oyas'in!" The phrase means, "All My Relations," and is the rough equivalent of "Amen." It ends our prayers and punctuates the passing of the Sacred Pipe. Shouted during the Inipi, it means the round is over and open the door pronto. Indian religion is practiced in the name of all our relations: the Earth, the Sky, the Winged Ones, The Four Leggeds, The Crawling Things, The Fins, and the Two Leggeds of all races. "Mitakuye Oyas'in" is our way of saying that we include ourselves in the world rather than exerting dominion over it.

Once the men were seated and the heated stones passed into the lodge, a bucket of water was handed to Whitewolf. Another Indian had been assigned to support me in my novitiate at door keeping. He would teach me the ropes as the ceremony proceeded. Together, we shut the door flap, sealing the lodge so tightly that not a speck of light could penetrate it. Immediately, I heard the splash of water hiss violently on the hot stones. Whitewolf's prayers segued to songs punctuated with the moans and groans of men suffering under intense heat. I plastered my ear to the canvas not wanting to miss a word from inside, and determined to open the door immediately on signal.

On the call, "Mitakuye Oyas'in," we wrenched up the door and a gust of hot steam seared my face. "Good God," I thought, "That's incredibly hot." Peering inside, I saw the participants pouring sweat, lying like puppies around the stone pit. The Inipi had completed its first round. There were three more to go. By the ceremony's end I doubted my chances to survive the ordeal, but was determined to try.

The Inipi finished, everyone piled out of the lodge and ran for the creek where they plunged their steaming bodies into the icy water. "Oh Lord," I thought. "That's plain crazy. They could have a heart attack."

Cooled down, dried, and dressed, the men headed for the house, while the women prepared their own sweatlodge. Two sets of stones had been heated at the same time, but men and women never used to sweat together. While mixed sweats are typical today, Whitewolf followed the old ways. Men and women pray differently, and they do better in separate sweats.

Inside the house, the men gossiped and waited until the women's Inipi was over. Then everyone gathered around a long table filled with cold cuts, cheeses, breads and salad. Every Sweatlodge ceremony concluded with a communal feast provided by the participants.

I was surprised to discover that Whitewolf often had a cadre of Indians living at his home. Flying in from South Dakota, they would stay with him until their business in Washington, DC was completed. He would feed, house, and see to their needs. In addition, there were always several people living permanently with him. Even though he was sometimes abused by freeloaders, he never turned anyone away.

The following week, I appeared at Whitewolf's Paradise ready for my virgin Inipi. With a generous measure of trepidation I helped prepare the lodge. Too soon, the stones were ready. We undressed and wrapped up for the ceremony. Rather than use a beach towel, I cunningly brought a sheet blanket which would cover more than a towel. It could shield me from head to foot if the steam was overwhelming.

We assumed our places in the lodge. A shallow pit at our feet occupied the central portion. Glowing red stones were piled into the hole. The bucket was handed in. Cedar and sage dropped onto the stones produced a cleansing smudge. Then, the door was sealed and I waited in the pitch blackness of my first Inipi.

A dipper of water had blasted us with steam, but Whitewolf continued to throw water on the stones until the skin on my face threatened to peel. I soon pulled the blanket over my head and lay down where it was slightly cooler, a bit more tolerable.

Just when I thought the first round was finished and the door would be opened, Larry Redshirt, Whitewolf's Oglala Indian brother, began another song. Inwardly I groaned with despair, but kept silent. Others were groaning out loud. The first round tends to be the hottest because the stones are not cooled at all. It is usually a short round unless someone from the Reservation is sweating. That being the case, a chance for a quick, hot round is nil. These young Lakotas love to sweat hot and long with no mercy on themselves or anyone else. When they were around, we all knew to hunker down for a "real" sweat. Wrapped up from head to toe in my sheet blanket, and groveling on the ground, I managed to endure the first round. The door opened a few moments and blessed, cool air wafted into the lodge. A bit of water was passed among us.

Too soon, the door was sealed and the second round began. During this round everyone prayed. When it was my turn, I managed to stammer a public prayer, but inwardly, I begged the Creator for simple survival. The lodge may have been a few degrees cooler, but with twelve men praying, it lasted forever. Once again, I was on the ground gasping for the tender mercies of Grandmother Earth. "Mitakuye Oyas'in!" and I was saved from heat prostration once again.

A little more water and some luscious fresh air gave way to the third round. Fresh stones were brought in! Someone had a question for the Spirits. This called for a super hot round with Whitewolf consulting the Spirits on behalf of the questioner. Having lasted this long, I began to dream of surviving the entire ceremony. Once again the doors were lifted and water shared.

The last round found Whitewolf offering his own prayers. It was the "going home" round. The stones were cooler, the atmosphere more gentle. When it was over, the Sacred Pipes were lit and their smoke carried our prayers upward to the Creator.

The Inipi completed, I fell out the door and lay panting in the grass before heading for the creek. The others were already splashing about when I tentatively stuck my toe in the cold water, a painful contrast to the steamy lodge. I had endured my first Inipi Ceremony. Six months later I was still wrapping myself in the sheet blanket during sweatlodge when Whitewolf finally ordered, "The next time you come here, leave your blanket at home, wear a towel, and sit up like everyone else!"

I replied with a weak, "Hau."

One Saturday several weeks later, it rained all afternoon. This did not stop the sweats. Fires can be built and maintained in a rain storm. I have only known one sweatlodge fire to be washed out. On this afternoon, a single fire tender remained outside. Everyone else had jammed into the house.

Suddenly, furniture was being shoved aside and a buffalo blanket spread on the floor. Whitewolf fished a rock, a box of needles and a package of single edge razor blades from a special bundle. Taking a large bunch of sage, he carefully smudged himself and the room. Then, filling his Chanunpa Wakan (Sacred Pipe) he placed it on the blanket according to Oglala Lakota tradition, stem facing West. So far as I know, the Oglalas are the only people whose ceremonies face West, the direction of Visions and Spiritual Power. All other Indian groups face their ceremonies East toward the sunrise and the new day. Not knowing what to expect, I waited.

One of the men knelt on the blanket, Whitewolf beside him. I whispered to the person next to me, "What are they doing?"

He answered, "Joe's giving flesh."

I wondered what that meant but said nothing. Whitewolf wiped the man's arm with sage. Then he pricked Joe's skin, lifted it slightly, and slid the razor under the needle cleanly lifting off a tiny square of flesh. A drop of blood immediately pooled over the wound and began to flow down Joe's arm. Whitewolf took another piece just above the first cut and repeated the action until seven flesh offerings had been taken from each of Joe's arms. Fourteen flesh offerings were secured in a small square of cloth to be burned in the sacred fire.

"Why did he do that?" I wanted to know.

Whitewolf overheard my question and replied, "When you are praying about something important or you are about to do something significant, you offer your flesh as a sign of your commitment. Think about it. The only thing you own that you can give to the Creator is your body. He has no need of your money. Everything else is His anyway. Your flesh is the most perfect offering you can make." Giving flesh accompanied all serious events.

The Sacred Pipe formed the heart of Whitewolf's Paradise. No serious undertaking was considered without first praying with the Pipe. Never handled with nonchalance, it was treated with the greatest reverence and respect. The Pipe was filled while kneeling barefooted. Only a special, sacred tobacco/herb mix was smoked. Outsiders may suspect that marijuana is smoked in our Pipes, but we never dishonored our most sacred object with dope.

Inipi ceremonies were usually held on Thursday evenings and Saturday afternoons unless Whitewolf was attending Sun Dance in South Dakota. Twice a week I drove to Paradise for ceremony. After a year, I asked if he would consecrate my Indian Pipe in the Inipi. I wanted to be a Pipe Carrier. Whitewolf agreed. The little Pipe I had found in Phoenix was properly blessed and became affectionately known as "Smokes Forever." It never seemed to burn out of tobacco no matter how many smoked it in the sacred circle.

While anyone can purchase an Indian Pipe, a Chanunpa, the wise will treat it with respect. First it should be smudged with sage, then used for personal prayers. If it is taken into the Sweatlodge and dedicated by an authorized person, it becomes a Sacred Pipe or Chanunpa Wakan. To have such a Pipe requires preparation, commitment to use it for the people; to conduct Pipe Ceremonies as needed and to generally assume responsibility within the community. It takes time to become a Pipe Carrier. One grows into the job. He or she is a servant of the people.

Within the year after taking up the Sacred Pipe, I stood on the Hill in my first Vision Quest, and soon thereafter, Whitewolf assigned me to run my first Sweatlodge. I had been through many by then. Running one should have been second nature for me. However, I was so anxious that I could barely remember the sequence of the ceremony. My buddies, affectionately supportive, joined me in the lodge, a rather courageous act on their parts. All that I remember of the structure of the Inipi ceremony was being blitzed out of my mind. I was totally lost in an altered state of consciousness, but I somehow led the ceremony. Laughing in between rounds, White-wolf would remind me what was coming next.

Once I settled into "pouring the waters," Whitewolf entrusted me with running the women's Sweatlodges when no woman was available for the task. He hated to run women's sweats.

"Duncan," he explained, "When a man cries in my sweatlodge, I understand why, but them women cry and I never know what's going on."

I enjoyed leading the women's Inipis. I liked the way they prayed, the honesty and sensitivity of their prayers. My only problem came from little girls. They pray forever, and when the lodge is shimmering in one hundred seventy-five degree heat, it is hard to endure while they remind the Creator of Martha's tabby cat who got hurt last week, and the oak tree down on the corner which was hit by lightning, and Kathy whose father keeps putting her on restrictions. . . . Soon the whole lodge would be on the ground crying, while these beautiful children, apparently immune to the heat, would pray ad infinitum.

Four-year-old Tsanina loved the Inipi. During the ceremony, no matter how hot it became, Tsanina would cuddle down behind her mother and shut her eyes. By the ceremony's end, she would be blissfully asleep as we fished her tiny body from the lodge. Little girls bless the ceremony with their innocence, sweetness, and endurance.

The day arrived, unbeknownst to me, that I was ready for new responsibilities. Whitewolf determined I should begin to take flesh.

He had pledged one hundred pieces and ordered me to take them from him.

He unrolled his blanket near the sweatlodge and filled his Pipe. The razor blade, needle, and sage waited ominously for me. White-wolf knelt down. Lifting his Pipe in prayer, he steeled himself for me to begin. My hand shook as I aimed the needle at his arm. Jabbing it in, I was dismayed to find his hide Rhinoceros tough. I finally hooked enough skin to take the first cut, but didn't make it all the way. Though the piece was lost, the cut bled profusely. I moved up to the next spot. At that point, Whitewolf was in serious prayer and I didn't blame him. I felt like a palsied version of Jack The Ripper. Suddenly, I realized that my vision was blurry. Without my reading glasses, I couldn't really see what I was doing.

"Just a moment, Bro," I stammered. Dropping the razor and needle, I bolted across the yard toward my truck.

Whitewolf, realizing that something was amiss, looked up and saw me disappearing in the distance. Dismayed, he yelled, "Duncan, where are you going?"

"To get my glasses," I hollered over my shoulder.

Moments later I resumed the surgery. After what seemed an eternity, I finished taking fifty pieces off his right arm and crawled to the other side where I cut another fifty. By the time I was finished we were both exhausted. I have seen Whitewolf take a lot of flesh. Since then I have taken hundreds of pieces myself, and I have given many. Today, both my arms are scarred from these small offerings. Non-Indians think this is a terribly primitive and ugly ritual. It is not. While somewhat bloody, it is not particularly painful, and it is a holy time of self offering. Most tribes have similar ceremonies although done in different ways. The Sun Dance for example, is a well known ceremony in which the dancers have their chests pierced. Our religion is not antiseptic nor is it for the squeamish.

I spent a total of seven years with Whitewolf before he released me to establish my own camp. At his camp I found my spiritual home. A

Monacan/Sioux spiritual leader, George Whitewolf, became "uncle" (special teacher) to me. Slowly, he guided my steps onto the Red Road and shaped my attitudes with his teaching. And it was in Whitewolf's care, exactly four years after my vision of the blue water, the golden light, and the number four, that I climbed the hill for my first Vision Quest. In many ways those years with Whitewolf were the most important of my life. I learned the ways of ceremony. I accepted responsibility in the Indian community. I came to know my Indian self and was accepted by my brothers and sisters as Indian.

By the end of the first year with Whitewolf my growing involvement in Indian life and ceremonies rendered impossible the continuation of my third marriage, which was with a woman named Sarah. She could not join me on my Indian path. Her personal integrity would not countenance her playing at a religion which she did not believe or hanging out with people she disliked.

In 1979 we divorced.

How Men and Women Found Each Other

Traditional Blood-Piegan Tale

Grandfather laughed with delight at His wonderful creation. All the grasses, trees, and animals occupied the spaces He had designed for them. But suddenly, Grandfather recognized a serious omission. The world was perfect in every way but one.

He had placed all the men in a village to the West and all the women in a separate village to the East. Clearly, with four days journey between them, the men and women would never get together. If they failed to find each other, the human beings would become extinct in one generation.

Grandfather puzzled over the situation. The two sexes had to meet. Moreover, play and pleasure had to permeate the meeting or men would never bother with it. The problem of the separate villages required serious consideration. Finally, Grandfather hit on a wonderful plan so creative that He decided to join the men, become Chief of their village, and personally implement the scheme.

After some time had passed, Grandfather recounted to the men a dream in which he had seen strange human beings called women. These two-leggeds lived four days journey to the East. Grandfather insisted that his dream was true.

Up to that time the men had lived contentedly in their village. They dressed in crude rawhide skins, and sheltered in simple brush arbors. The men hunted with bows and arrows and had plenty to eat. The men felt they had everything they needed, but the old Chief was so excited about the new human beings in his dream that the men agreed to investigate. They commissioned their best scout to surreptitiously locate the strangers' village. He journeyed four days eastward, and to his surprise, stumbled upon the women's camp. Hiding in the bushes, he spent a whole day observing these new human beings and their fine lodges. These two-leggeds wore beautifully tanned buckskins. Their long hair shone in the sun. Ornaments decorated their ears and hung from their necks.

These new human beings were interesting in other ways as well. Their bodies were shaped differently: softer, curvaceous, and mysterious, not at all like men's bodies. Fascinated, he felt enchanted by these strangers.

Melting back into the forest, the scout raced home to give a full report. Awed by his descriptions of their clothing and lodges, the men were even more curious about the soft, rounder, mysterious bodies he depicted.

In the meantime, the old woman chief had discovered large moccasin tracks outside her village, footprints that obviously didn't belong to any of the women. Intrigued by what manner of two-legged had been spying on them, the Old Woman chief instructed her best scout to follow the tracks and report back on what she found.

The woman scout tracked four days westward until she suddenly detected a very strange camp. The lodges were so primitive that they offered little shelter, and the filthy two-leggeds of this village did not know how to dress.

It was an ugly camp but with one important exception; these two leggeds had weapons with which to hunt. The women hunted by driving buffalo over a cliff, and harvesting the meat, bones, and hides. But, these strange two-leggeds did not require a buffalo jump, as they apparently hunted with bows, arrows, and spears, weapons unknown to the women's village.

The strange two-leggeds were different in other ways as well, fascinatingly different. They were hard and lean. Their bodies sported big muscles. They swaggered, and they had something else that she had never seen before dangling between their legs. With no idea of its use, it compelled her attention.

After seeing enough, she slipped back into the forest and returned to her village. She described all that she had seen and the womens' eyes danced with wonder and excitement.

In the meantime, Grandfather chief was piquing the men's curiosity about women. Before long, he suggested, "Why don't we pay these novel human beings a visit? Maybe they have something we would like." The men grunted assent and early the next morning all the men began their trek through the woods toward the women's village. After four days, the men gathered at the edge of the woods, staring down at the women's camp, and pondered what to do next.

That very day the women had been talking about the strangers to the west, excited by the possibility of meeting these new human beings, hoping they might visit and hunt game for them.

Suddenly, a woman scout alerted her sisters that the woods were full of strangers. Immediately, the women jerked on their finest buckskin dresses, yanked combs through their hair, hung shells in their ears and bone necklaces around their necks. In record time, the women gathered in a line outside their village to welcome the newcomers.

But when the men stepped out of the woods, eager to meet their neighbors, the women were appalled at the sight before them. These strangers smelled! They were grungy! They didn't know how to dress! These ugly, stinking two-leggeds would never be allowed in the women's village. The old woman chief picked up a stone, bounced it off the old chief's head and yelled, "Go away." All the women began to hurl stones and shout, "Get away. Go home."

The men, stunned and hurt, fell back into the woods. They neither expected nor deserved that kind of mistreatment. Grandfather chief rubbed the knot on his head and muttered, "Let's go home." Disappointed and disgruntled, the men retreated to their village. Grandfather's plan was falling apart. If it couldn't be resurrected, this would be the end of the human beings. Grandfather had another idea.

Calling the men together, he urged them to dare contacting the women creatures one more time. He herded the men into the river, taught them how to wash their bodies and untangle their hair. He commanded them to don their best rawhide loin cloths. When the men were clean and assembled, they began their second journey eastward but with a little trepidation.

This time, the men arrived at the women's village on the day of the buffalo jump. When the woman scout reported that the strangers had returned, the women agreed to meet the men but stayed dressed in their work clothes thinking that would equalize the situation. The women assembled, dressed in buckskins stiff with buffalo blood, their hair greasy and splattered with buffalo guts. They looked like an evil band of cannibal spirits.

When the men caught sight of the women, they bolted in terror for the woods and raced homeward. Grandfather was distraught, his finest plan thwarted at every turn.

The old woman chief pondered the situation. Maybe, she ought to give these odd strangers another chance. True, the strangers were a cruddy lot, but they could hunt and feed the whole camp. During their last encounter the strangers seemed more acceptable.

Calling her people together, the old woman chief proposed that they visit the men's village and assure the men that no harm had been intended. The women spent hours getting ready, dressing in their best clothes, adorning their hair, and ornamenting themselves with their finest jewelry. Then, they headed westward.

A hunter encountered them when they were but a day away from the men's camp. He tore back to the village to warn the men of this impending visit. The old man chief commanded, "Quick, all of you, into the river." The men scrubbed as best they could, pulled the tangles out of their hair, donned their finest rawhide loin cloths, and gathered in line awaiting the women's arrival.

The two groups eyed each other with both caution and fascination. The Grandfather chief whispered to his men, "Let me do the talking." He approached the old woman chief. She stepped forward and raised her hand in greeting.

The Grandfather offered, "Would you like to talk?"

The old woman chief responded, "Okay."

"Maybe we should go off in the woods alone to talk," he observed.

She responded, "Why not?"

When they found a private spot, He asked, "Are you interested in doing something that has never been done before?"

The woman chief agreed, "I guess so."

Grandfather chief suggested, "Maybe we should do this lying down."

"Fine," assented the old woman chief.

A few moments later lying in the grass, big grins splitting their faces, the woman chief enthused, "That was outrageous. Better than buffalo tongue!"

The old man chief said, "It was good for me too. Maybe we better go and tell the others. I think they'll like it." But, when they emerged from the woods, arms around each other's waists, not a man or woman was in sight. They were all in the woods doing what had never been done before.

Soon, the men moved into the women's village. Before long, men and women were falling in love. Before long, they were getting married, and soon they were having babies.

Grandfather chief sighed, "That's more like it," and He returned to His place above the world, charmed by his children below.

Committed to Marriage

1979 – Maryland

In late 1978 I first met Priscilla. Within the year I knew I had at last found my soul mate, my eternal love.

The opportunity finally arrived for my introduction to Priscilla's mother. Her father was not yet ready to participate in this event. But, Mom had no preconceptions. She invited me for lunch to reach her own conclusions.

Arriving at Priscilla's parental home in Bethesda, Maryland, we repaired to the kitchen where Mom was tossing the salad. Leaning back against the counter, I observed the two women fussing over the meal until Mom abruptly stopped the world with *the question.* Fixing me with her clear blue eyes, Priscilla's mother asked the one question for which I had no good answer. "Her father and I want to know why you have been married and divorced three times."

There were no hidden agendas. She did not talk around the issue nor prejudge my moral character. I thought it wonderfully refreshing to meet this mother who could ask *the question* so clearly and without malice or prejudice. She really wanted to know about this man who had failed at three marriages and now wanted her daughter to be his fourth. I was charmed by her honesty. I would have asked the same question were I in her shoes.

Searching for an answer, my mind raced back to my first marriage. I had fallen in love with Rose during the early weeks of our freshman year in college. We were both young but knew our hearts. I was nineteen and she was twenty when we married. We stayed together seventeen years and proudly produced three daughters and one son.

Like me, Rose had dedicated her life to the ministry and was a religion major in college. We shared that passion for a decade, but as we matured we developed conflicting interests. After seventeen years, I dared to contemplate breaking out of the marriage and living free. The late 1960's exuded the spirit of Coyote and I reveled under his tutelage.

Falling headlong in love with Maria, I plunged into a new marriage which was ill fated from the beginning. We were in such different stages of life and with such incompatible needs, the marriage never had a chance. The one lovely outcome of our union was the adoption of Christina, whose big brown baby eyes enchanted everyone she met.

When I left Rose, I packed all my personal possessions in a tiny Fiat Spider sports car. When I left Maria, everything was crammed into a Pinto station wagon. It took a U Haul Truck to carry my belongings when Sarah and I split. I tease Priscilla that if we don't make it, I will call Mayflower Van Lines. She laughs because she knows there is no danger that I would ever leave her.

I stood in Mom's kitchen, back pressed against the counter, trying to think what I could say that wouldn't be self-serving. Could I attribute the mess I made of my marriages to Coyote? Certainly, the Trickster had teamed up with my own Coyote nature to encourage my matrimonial proclivities. Should I say "The devil made me do it?"

No matter what had influenced me, I was responsible for my behavior, so, I chose to recount my family history. Both of my grandmothers had been married four times. The family had boasted that we, indeed, had "fore-fathers," and I joked that it was incumbent on me to keep that tradition alive.

Then with a laugh I said aloud what I knew in my soul to be true. "Priscilla and I will never divorce." She is number four. Tradition has been fulfilled. I finally got it right. And with a brave smile I quietly added. . . . "And it certainly proves one thing. I *am* committed to the institution of marriage."

Strawberries

A Traditional Cherokee Tale

Long, long ago when the earth was complete and all the nations of animals and plants had been colonized on this continent, the time came to settle the first man and woman into their new home. Grandfather established them in the heart of the Great Smoky Mountains where, surrounded by berries, nuts, plants and plentiful game, life would be easy.

The first man and the first woman delighted in each other that initial year. Very little work was required of them. Brief hunting forays provided enough meat. All the necessary plants could be gathered with minimal effort. Mostly the two human beings spent long hours together talking, making love, and discovering their new world.

Sometime, in the second year, the woman noticed that her husband was beginning to irritate her. He was under-foot too much. She hated to admit it, but he could be lazy. She tried to keep these observations to herself most of the time. The man and woman truly loved each other in spite of the small aggravations.

By the third year, minor vexations had become major. Quarrels developed between them, evolving into verbal rages. By the end of the year, they battled constantly. She nagged him all the time, and the more she complained, the more mulish he became. One morning they had hardly cleared the bed when a particularly nasty argument ensued. Names and curses flashed like lightning bolts. Furious, the woman vowed to leave. She had enough of him for a lifetime. Heading for the door, she lunged down the path going east. "Never," she vowed, "will I return to this lodge and gaze on your ugly face. I'm out of here!"

"Good riddance!" he shouted after her. "Maybe I can have some peace now!" And he muttered to himself, "Goldarn woman! She'd nag the warts off a bull frog. I hope she keeps her word and stays gone."

All that day, the woman rushed down the eastward path. With her jaw thrust out and her facial muscles working, she glared straight ahead.

Her moccasins slapped the ground like angry hands pounding bread dough. She would not be deterred.

In the meantime, the man was lying in his hammock relaxing, basking in the peacefulness. He had never known the pleasure of a quiet house where no bossy woman constantly scolded him. That evening there was plenty of left-over food for him to eat. Admittedly, the bed was rather lonely, but not lonely enough for him to want the shrew back.

The next morning he awoke to a barren house. Loneliness replaced the quiet, and the silence reflected the emptiness in his heart. Grudgingly, he realized he missed her. By night fall, his misery so overwhelmed him that he was oblivious to the hunger in his belly. In bed, the hunger of his loins tormented him; he grieved over the loss of his woman. The man wailed and sobbed and felt sorry for himself.

Not once since leaving home had the woman slowed her pace. The second nightfall found her still stomping on the eastward path, moccasins resounding in the quiet forest, her clenched jaw leading the way, her rage like a roaring fire. She would kiss a pig before she ever touched him again!

Grandfather listened to the weeping of the man who was growing more pitiful by the moment. Finally, Grandfather asked, "Do you really miss her?"

"Oh yes, Grandfather, I miss her so very much," sobbed the man.

"If I get her back for you, will you be good to her?"

"Oh yes, Grandfather, I will be good to her. I'll do everything for her. She will never have to ask for anything again," cried the man.

"Okay, I'll see what I can do."

Grandfather spied the woman still obstinately tromping down the road. Grandfather could see that He had to slow up her progress so that the man could catch up with her. The man was running pell mell down the path, stumbling and falling, desperate to reach his beloved.

Grandfather considered the options. He didn't want to strong-arm the woman by forcing her to go back. He had hoped to facilitate her wanting to return to the marriage. This would take some serious strategy.

Grandfather recognized that the woman must be hungry. She had not stopped for food or drink since she left home. So Grandfather deposited a clump of the finest ripe huckleberries in front of her, but the woman blew by them without a notice. Farther on the path he placed a blackberry bush loaded with succulent fruit. She glanced at them but did not waiver, so strong did the anger still burn inside her. One after the other, Grandfather positioned berry bushes and fruit trees in her path to no avail.

Clearly, Grandfather would have to work great magic if he was to slow down this angry woman. He thought and thought until finally He knew just what to do.

He created a fruit, juicy, red, and shaped like a heart, and he covered two acres of ground with this temptation. Her path led straight through the beautiful fruit patch; surely she would not be able to resist this temptation. All the while, the man was rushing down the road behind her, praying to catch up.

When the woman entered the trap, she was entranced by the bright, juicy redness of the fruit. She slowed to look but vowed not to eat. Nothing would deter her escape from that lazy good-for-nothing back home. But the more she looked at the fruit the hungrier she became until finally she paused to sample just one.

Putting it in her mouth, she was transfixed by its juicy sweetness. *Well, maybe one more,* and that one led to another and another, until finally she squatted and stuffed her mouth. The luscious red juice trickled down her chin.

Slowly a thought began to form in her mind, *I bet my man would like these.* She smiled, and it was her first smile of many days. Making a basket of her skirt, she began to fill it with the fruit. A happy tune hummed in her throat as she picked.

At that very moment the man crested the hill and spotted his woman in the field ahead. He froze. Every man knows instinctively never to rush at an angry woman. Safety requires that he check things out first, see how she feels, survey the lay of the land. Thus, the man watched carefully to determine his course of action.

The woman saw him standing tentatively in the road. She smiled and motioned him to approach, and when he reached her, she lifted a perfect fruit and placed it in his mouth. It burst with goodness and flavor. Oh, how wonderful it tasted! She fed him another and another until finally, he put his arm around her shoulder and turned her gently back toward their lodge.

The old Cherokee people say that Grandfather created strawberries to be the first fruit of Springtime so that when human beings are cranky from being locked up together all winter, strawberries will bring a smile to their faces and love back to their hearts.

Taking My Bride

1981 – Whitewolf's Place, Rural Maryland

"D uncan, go places with her. Sleep with her. Do whatever you want with her, but don't marry her. There has been too much mixing of our blood with the Whites. We have to marry our own kind." White-wolf held strong opinions about intermarriage between Whites and Indians.

Adopting most of his attitudes on Indian/Anglo matters, I agreed with him about interracial marriage. Having been badly burned by white women who were embarrassed by my "religious fanaticism" or angered by my spending time with Indians, I was determined that should I marry again it would be to an Indian woman interested in the traditional religion. I fantasized about her. She would have long black hair, high cheekbones and big brown eyes. I deeply cared for a woman in Arizona and thought she might be the one. She possessed all the required attributes, but when I met Priscilla in Maryland, the clarity of my prejudices was clouded by the reality of my love.

My path crossed with Priscilla's when I decided to leave academia for work in the clinical world. A mental health agency in Southern Maryland was advertising for an Executive Director. I applied and was invited for an interview with both the Board of Directors and the Clinical Director. On the appointed day I waited in an outer office. Finally, they summoned me into an inner sanctum where I found myself face to face with seven men and two women. The younger of the two ladies, the Clinical Director, stammered, "I thought you were a woman" and immediately spilled her notebooks and papers on the floor. I flippantly replied, "The last time I checked, I was still a man."

I got the job. The klutzy female interviewer was Priscilla. Her befuddlement during my interview did not predict her total focus in the office. An energetic individual, Priscilla eluded my attempts to discuss treatment philosophy and agency commitments. She was eternally supervising her staff, plowing through files, or running to meetings.

I complained to my financial administrator that I needed time to talk with my Clinical Director, but she never stood still long enough. I was aching with curiosity about this woman.

My chance emerged a month later when she and I drove to a nearby town for an inter-agency meeting. Relaxing and recounting humorous stories, we shared a wonderful break from our hectic schedules. One absurd story led to another. I told her the true tale of a priest who appeared in a Baltimore Hospital emergency room with a light bulb wedged up his rectum. Priscilla launched into the song, "You light up my life." The song turned out to be a metaphor. The image of the priest, the ridiculous song, the conviviality of storytelling and laughter eased our relationship. Priscilla began to light up my life as no one had ever done before.

Having been raised by two physicians, an agnostic mother and an atheist father, to hold science as a religion, she was spiritually hungry. To her astonishment, Native American symbols and motifs were emerging in her dreams. Turning to her Jungian Analyst, she was encouraged to explore the dreams by participating in the sacred ceremonies of the American Indian.

She was eager to partake in sweatlodge and Pipe ceremonies, but it was important that Priscilla avoid Whitewolf's camp so that the professional nature of our relationship be preserved. The intensity of sacred ceremony might involve us in more personal intimacy than would be appropriate or comfortable for either of us at that time. So, I arranged for her to attend Sweatlodges and Lakota ceremonies in a neighboring Indian camp.

Week by week, in spite of our precautions, our feelings for each other grew stronger. She was everything I admired in a woman; bright, professional, strong, witty, and growing in her commitment to the red road. But, there was a major problem. She was full blooded Irish-American. Rendered nonplused by my feelings, I confided my dilemma to Whitewolf who counseled, "Play with her, have sex with her. Every man needs a woman for that. Just don't marry her."

That evening in the sweatlodge I asked Whitewolf to beseech the Spirits for advice about Priscilla. My psyche was rent by conflicting allegiances. Until I met her, I was certain that if I married again, it would be to an indian woman. Now I was confused.

Whitewolf prayed, "Hau Grandfather! Sings-Alone here wants to know what to do about his white woman friend." More water was poured on the rocks making the lodge intensely hot. The participants hunkered down, moaned, and sang a Pipe song, while Whitewolf grunted through a one-sided conversation with the Spirits.

Whitewolf almost choked as he reported, "The Spirits say that you must not play around with that woman. She is a good woman who deserves better than that. If you sleep with her, you marry her."

My heart jumped inside me as I inwardly cried, "Thank you. Thank you, Grandfather."

I told Whitewolf that I wanted to bring Priscilla for the next sweatlodge ceremony. He agreed. Truth to tell, he was intrigued by this Irish-American woman who had stolen my heart. The next week when we arrived at Whitewolf's camp, Priscilla departed to split wood for the sweatlodge fire, one of her favorite forms of physical exercise. In the meantime, I searched in the house for Whitewolf and a cup of coffee.

After he and I gossiped a bit, he asked, "Where is that woman you were going to bring?"

"She is down at the wood pile," I couldn't hide my glee at Whitewolf's skepticism. A wood-chopping woman did not compute for him.

Hoisting himself out of his over-stuffed chair, Whitewolf trundled over to the window and stared, transfixed. What a treat watching Whitewolf watching Priscilla, not believing his eyes. Turning to me incredulously, he exclaimed, "Goddamn, Duncan! She swings an axe like a man". Suddenly being Irish-American was not so bad.

Months later, I prayed in the sweatlodge about wanting to marry this white woman. Would Whitewolf do the ceremony if the Spirits approved the marriage? The Spirits confirmed that Priscilla and I belonged together and ordered Whitewolf to perform the wedding.

The big day arrived. We had worked hard to fulfill tradition. Priscilla ground corn meal by hand. I jerked buffalo meat and seasoned it for a day in hickory smoke. Then I ground the jerky with dried berries and raisins, seasoning it with rendered fat, to make pemmican. Central to the traditional wedding ceremony was feeding ground corn and pemmican to each other and to the community. The long, exciting hours spent in preparation assured a joyful day of ceremony and feast. We delighted in our Jewish friends making Indian fry bread and enjoyed the odd mixture of guests: Christians, Jews, Traditional Indians, Lawyers, Doctors, High school graduates.

Whitewolf fashioned us each a beautiful outfit; mine was of fine, beaded, white elk skin. Priscilla sported a beautiful, tan elk skin dress with knee high moccasins.

Family, friends and Indian community gathered outside near the sweatlodge, waiting for the procession of Whitewolf, Priscilla, and myself from the house. Whitewolf inspected Priscilla, grinned widely, and announced, "Now you look like a proper Lakota woman!" Flush with Irish pride and mischief, she retorted "I love the traditional dress you made me, but you need to know that underneath, in honor of my Irish ancestors, I am wearing Kelly green underwear."

Whitewolf scowled, muttering in Lakota, "Crazy white woman."

The Lady Dreams

If you were my gardener, oh
What a garden we would grow!

With wildflowers at the centre
In bursts of gold and blues
The dappling of the sun and sky
In ancient riming hues,

In shadow, eight shy peonies
And thirty daisies too
To celebrate each wakening day
Hung deep in morning dew,

And languid ivy trails you'd plant
To lead me quick to you.

If you were my gardener, oh
What a garden we would grow!

—Priscilla Cogan

North

The color is red.

North brings us strength, endurance and healing.
It is a time of cleansing and purification.
For Indian people, North is associated
with the bitter cold of Winter
which is a time of suffering,
even dying.
But they also saw strength, renewal and healing come
from the rigors of this powerful season.
The following stories are illustrative
of both the hard and scary times in my evolution,
but also the healings which came to and through me.

North is represented by
the Buffalo Nation.

Facing North: The Third Vision Quest; Thunder Beings

1981 – Again, Whitewolf's Vision Quest Hill

Now it was June a year later, and the permanent donut worn into my altar bore mute testimony to the crawling, sucking, craziness of my previous Hanblecheya. Having sworn never to submit to another Vision Quest, I was nevertheless preparing for three days and three nights on the hill.

This time I suffered no illusions about my handling Vision Quests. Only the Spirits could shepherd me through three days and nights of Hanblecheya. Accurately assessing my own spiritual inadequacy, I admitted my inability to survive the coming Hanblecheya alone.

I dreaded the third trip to the hill, but yearned to complete my Vision. The Grandfathers had granted me my name and medicine. I had learned my lesson about patience. But I needed clarification of the Vision which suggested that I link traditional American Indians with assimilated urban Indians wanting to "come home."

So, repeating the usual preparations, I found myself once again in my altar with no shelter, food, water, or faith in myself. This time I selected a spot containing two, tiny tulip poplar saplings about four feet tall. They gave precious little shade but did provide me a small sun screen.

The first day and night dragged by. I prayed, watched, waited, and dodged the sun. During the night, between prayers, I slept dreamlessly. The second day was sunny but pleasant. All afternoon I held my Pipe and snuggled beneath the small poplars. I cherished those little trees.

Evening gathered and then darkness fell. Periodically I would hear the community sing or would smell the sweatlodge smoke. Thirst preempted my consciousness and I prayed to survive. I knew that Priscilla was fasting food and water with me even while splitting wood and praying in the sweatlodge each day. She was suffering physically more than I. All that was required of me was to watch and pray. Remembering her, I felt ashamed of my weakness.

The night eased by without event; no Visions, no dreams, no visitations . . . nothing. But patiently I bided my time. Never again would I challenge the Creator. Other than for weakness, hunger, and dehydration, I was okay.

The third night opened on a very quiet Vision Quest. This Hanblecheya was providing a simple, comparatively easy time to reflect and pray. Of course all that was about to change.

Faint rumblings shook the distant stillness. A certain foreboding tensed the hill. The Creation seemed to hunker down expectantly. Then distant flashes lit the sky beyond the horizon, giving substance to the thunder. I watched with apprehension as the storm advanced. Checking my altar to be assured that all was ready, I covered my blanket with the deer hide, hoping for a dry bed later.

The first breezes caressed me with blessed coolness. The winds increased as the lightning flashed nearer. Racing clouds hid the moon so that my altar fluctuated between the pitch black of night and the blazing brightness of lightning.

Then the storm attacked the hill. I was dazzled by the brilliant lightning flashing against the black night. The air smelled of ozone. It seemed the lightning was licking the hill in search of Vision Quester flesh. Standing my ground, Pipe uplifted, I begged the Thunder Beings for pity.

As if responding to my prayer, the clouds opened. A deluge flooded the hill. Water poured over me. Every pore of my body opened to drink the moisture. Mouth agape and ignoring the lightning, I let the rain pelt my tongue. The crashing storm assaulted, struck, and flooded the hill as it built toward its inevitable climax. A warning flashed in my mind, *I am the highest thing up here.* Falling to my knees and rolling onto my side, I fervently clutched my Sacred Pipe and curled against the storm. Suddenly, all went black!

When I came to, the cosmic orgasm had resolved into relaxation and peace. The clouds had disappeared. Stars twinkled overhead in a deep clear sky. What an amazing transformation! Standing, I thanked the Grandfather, the Good Spirits and the Thunders for sparing me. I thanked Them for the tumultuous night. The Hanblecheya was drawing to a close. It had been a hell of an experience but I had endured. I could finally relax.

Not so fast! As if on command, legions of mosquitos attacked. Assaulting my sunburned flesh, they bit, tormented, and tortured me. I would wipe them away in a swath of broken and bloody fragments. Eaten alive, I couldn't persist any longer on the hill. Abandoning my altar, fleeing the blood-thirsty demons, I tore down the path toward the sweatlodge, Pipe and medicine bundle in my hands.

The now familiar cry, "He's down! He's down!" pierced the peace of the night. The sleepy community that had kept watch through the storm roused itself to kindle the sweatlodge fire and prepare for the final ceremony. Priscilla had been keeping vigil in the sweatlodge itself, so she exited as I entered. I could not look at her, shamed that I had been run off the hill again.

Once again there were no Visions, dreams or visitations to recount for the Spirits. No further instructions about my earlier Vision. Whitewolf wondered aloud how I could manage to stay on the hill during a blazing storm only to be chased off by a few harmless mosquitos.

Obviously, I had not a clue.

Gun Smoke

1973 – Eight years earlier, Colorado River Indian Tribes

As I look back upon those first months on the reservation, I realize how much I was tested by the Powers of the North. I remember so vividly the disappointment I felt upon my reservation arrival, the dawning awareness that living and working for the tribe would be fraught with struggle, the ambiguity with which I was received; all suggesting that my survival would require a great deal of endurance and no small amount of suffering.

During my third week on the reservation an urgent message commanded my immediate presence in the Treasurer's office. A woman had telephoned, threatening to shoot herself and her children. Gathered in the office was the Treasurer, the Director of Tribal Rehabilitation Programs, and the Tribal Police Chief. Obviously, it was up to the new shrink to save those innocent babies.

Testing time for me. If I insisted this was a law enforcement problem, the tribal leaders would label me a coward. If I intervened and got shot, at least no one important to the tribe would have been lost. If I was successful, I might be accepted as a man and a healer.

"Okay, I'll take care of it," was my reply, "But you'll have to show me where she lives. I still don't know my way around the reservation."

My inner tormentor snickered that my spiritual journey was about to be terminated by a smoking gun. I would die on a stranger's doorstep, all alone, thousands of miles from family and friends on a Mohave desert Indian reservation. Hopefully, someone here would share the jeopardy with me.

Wrong!

"Follow us and we will point out the house," was all the police chief offered. Their faces betrayed no interest in backing me up. The three of them piled into one subcompact car while I followed in the Pinto. Watching them I couldn't help but laugh. Mohaves are typically very large people. Many are morbidly obese. They drive either pickup trucks, jokingly called Navaho Cadillacs, or tiny subcompacts which suffer, wheels splayed, under their burdens. The small car bravely hauled its load in front of me. Slowing down at a cul de sac and leaning out the window, the chief pointed to a small frame house as the little car groaned away, abandoning me to the danger of an armed, demented woman. There was to be no back-up.

Taking a few deep breaths and assuring myself that this was a good day to die, hoping beyond hope that God wanted me alive tomorrow, I stepped out of the car, strode boldly to the house, and rapped on the door. It opened slightly. A woman peered through the crack. I knew her! She worked in the Tribal office building. Thank God, we were acquainted. Perhaps I would survive another day after all.

Her eyes puzzled, she grunted, "Hello."

Maintaining my most friendly and off-hand demeanor, I inquired, "Hey, how are you doing?"

"Okay." She waited.

No gun was evident and I was still alive. "Listen, I hate to bother you, but I was told that you have a gun and threatened to kill yourself and your children."

Her face broke into a broad smile, "Yeah, I really upset them, didn't I?" Her lidded eyes belied her laugh.

I wanted to get her away from the house into neutral territory, "Can someone watch your children a few minutes?"

"Yeah, my neighbor is here. Why?" She eyed me suspiciously.

"Let's go get a cup of coffee and talk about it."

When she agreed, I had mixed feelings—surprise, relief, and irritation. She couldn't be both imminently dangerous and willing to go with me. Was this just a sick, manipulative trick? There seemed no need for my terror. Still, I kept my eyes on her purse; she might be concealing a gun.

In an hour lubricated by coffee, she described her beef with a certain tribal official and assured me that she was not going to kill anyone. With the crisis passed, I had proved something to myself and, hopefully, to the Mohave leadership.

As I left her front door, she turned, smiled, "How about taking me dancing Saturday night?"

Crisis time again. I had no interest in dating her, especially with this recent history of threats. She had also become a client, precluding a social relationship. It was Coyote's favorite predicament.

I stammered that I didn't dance or frequent bars, but thanks anyway. She proved my lie when a month later she caught me dancing in a bar with a friend from back East. I held my breath, fearing a confrontation, but she let it pass.

Thank God for small favors. The spiritual walk is never simple or easy, and sometimes it can be deadly.

I Will Kill You

Christmas, 1974

V iolence constantly intruded into my world. Brutality lurked as the reservation's shadow. Alcohol was its catalyst and excuse. Many an offense was dismissed by, "He didn't mean any harm. He was drunk."

I did not know a single reservation family unscarred by alcohol. North American Indian tribes have no history of social drinking. Liquor was unknown until it was introduced by white merchants who used it to gain an edge over the usually savvy native traders. A bottle would be chugalugged in turn by all drinkers until good judgement vanished with the booze.

To this day, many Indian people drink quickly and with the single goal of drunkenness. I have often been challenged, "Why drink other than to get drunk?" Drunkenness exacerbates the hopelessness of many Native Americans who, tied to their land, cannot function in the cities but can find no real work at home. A drunken stupor numbs feelings of uselessness.

Many times I watched a circle of elderly alcoholics sharing a bottle under a tree near the hospital. Grandmother Earth received the first taste of Thunderbird wine. Then, once proud men anesthetized their despair by passing the bottle until all were drunk. Too often these comrades-in-wine degenerated into enemies fighting among themselves. Later, they would be treated at the hospital for cuts and contusions.

Once when I left the office, a drunk Lakota man blocked my way. John and I knew each other. We had previously spent social time together. Although he ordinarily claimed me as friend, on that day he wanted to fight. I managed to divert him. Another morning as I entered the bathroom, my nose nearly collided with a fist—another drunk. This one I enrolled in the hospital detox program.

Yet, another acquaintance once stormed into my office to do battle. He suffered from liver damage and was quite weak but eager to test his manhood by whipping the outsider. Week by week violence stalked me, experiences without precedent back East. I managed to escape each attack, but the worst was yet to come.

It was Christmas week. I had taken a few days of vacation and returned to find the alcoholism counselor nursing a broken nose. One of the Bradlee boys, a mountain of a man, had crashed the offices looking for me. When the counselor had stuck his head out the door to offer help, he was pulverized by a giant fist.

The next day I looked up from my desk to find the door blocked by the big guy himself.

He screwed up his face and snarled, "I'm gonna kill you."

I froze, my mind churning. There was no escape except through that door. I dared not reach for the phone, so I hunkered down and waited.

He lowered his eye brows menacingly, "I think I'll cut your fuckin' throat first."

I was watching warily, but what could I do? What do you say to a man who is twice your size, has a history of violence, is drunk as sin, and dead set on your termination?

He growled, "I'm gonna blow your ass up."

Clearly, I had to act to protect my rear and/or my throat.

"Yeah, I can tell you are furious with me and that you fully aim to break my neck, but before you kill me, how about telling me why. If I gotta go, I want to know what I've done." My statement caught him off guard, so I continued hopefully, "You're no fool. You wouldn't be threatening me without reason."

He relaxed a little.

Seizing the moment, I urged him, "Why don't you sit down here and tell me about it?"

To my surprise, he slumped into an empty chair.

My relief was awesome. Once he was off his feet, the battle was almost over. "What's happened," I asked calmly.

He began to explain, "I went down to the Tribal Chairman's office to get my allotment."

The Tribe collected rent from the huge truck farms occupying tribal lands, and this money, rightfully his, was distributed at year's end.

"The Tribal Chairman won't give me my money until you okay it."
He continued, "He says I'm too drunk to have my money and won't
give it to me, 'less you say so."

"Un Huh, go on." I listened, knowing I had to keep him talking.

"Well, it's my money and you got no say over it!"

Now the Tribal Chairman was obviously right to fear the money
being wasted, but it had been terribly unfair to put me in the middle. I
agreed with the man sitting before me. This was none of my business.
I told the man-mountain so and asked him to remove himself.

To my great relief, Bradlee trundled off down the hall with physical
mayhem still on his mind. Having saved my own skin, I phoned ahead
to warn the Chairman's office of their coming encounter.

Fortunately, he detoured by the bar for a beer to fortify himself
before facing the Tribal Chairman. When he threatened to blow up
the bar just for the hell of it, the tribal police intervened. The avenging
giant cooled off in a cell. The rest of the world relaxed for a while.

Building Defenses

1975 – On the reservation

I had always envied friends who lose their appetites to sickness or stress. Not me! When I am under pressure I turn to a Navaho Taco or a pastry. The pressure of those first experiences had taken it's toll. Month by month, as I struggled with reservation life, my waist ballooned until I could no longer wear my clothes. The final ego blow was delivered by a friend who wondered aloud how I managed to have sex, "being so fat and all."

It dawned on me that being overweight and out of shape might be inconsistent with survival when violence was a constant companion. Driven by self preservation and a bruised ego, I altered my eating habits and embarked on a jogging regimen. Purchasing some running shoes and a "How-To" running book, I found a secluded road which afforded me a quarter mile of level pavement. The first day I managed to walk and run a mile. By the end of the week I could run half a mile. Within a month, I ran several miles without stopping, and soon thereafter I was covering five to six miles in an hour, about 35 miles a week. The lard began to steadily melt away, and I felt better, safer and more self-confident. Considering that most Mohaves were also overweight, I figured I could outrun an attacker if necessary.

It occurred to me that if running was good, martial arts training would be even better. A karate studio had opened in Parker. One noon while having lunch with a friend, I suggested, "Let's see if we can get some private karate lessons. I'm not hot on joining a kids' class, but if we could have private lessons, just the two of us, it would be fun." To my delight he responded enthusiastically. We promptly enrolled and paid for a series of twelve sessions.

My friend wasn't nearly as obese as I, and he was a good bit taller. With his long hair and scraggly beard, he was a formidable looking gentleman. The two of us together must have created quite an impression. At the appointed time we showed up for class and began to grunt, groan, and punch our way toward a green belt. We were having fun. By golly, if I couldn't outrun an assailant, I might fetch a round-house kick which would send him flying. Of course, the attacker would have to stand very still. If he moved, I might strain a muscle or otherwise hurt myself. To enhance my karate fitness I added thirty knuckle pushups daily in addition to my jogging. Four weeks later we showed up for class, proud of our increasing prowess. Voila! A sign on the door said "Closed." Our black belt instructor had fled with our money, aborting two promising careers in the martial arts.

Feeling thoroughly ripped off, I put all my energy into jogging. Running in circles became my metaphor while Coyote served as a trail guide.

Healing

1973 – Colorado River Indian Tribes

If suffering and endurance come from the North, so does strength which leads to healing and purification. Having a vision does not guarantee that life will be easy. Mystics have suggested that the soul must be tested before true healing can occur. I saw this process unfold many times in Whitewolf's community, but more to the point, I experienced it in myself.

An Anglo doctor looks for a constellation of symptoms from which he or she makes a diagnosis and prescribes a cure. Usually, treatment aims at removing symptoms but typically ignores the life style and internal states which caused the illness in the first place. The Native American "doctor" is more concerned with the whole person, knowing that an illness can be wiped out, but if the patient is not changed, a new disease will manifest itself.

Until I entered upon the Red Road, I had made more than my share of stupid mistakes. I had been ridden mercilessly by the Coyote Spirit, embracing it all the while. I was out of balance. My value system was dictated by momentary desires and vanity. Healing for me was a slow process begun on the reservation. Not only was I enduring my own hard times, I was confronting suffering and spirit-sickness like I had never seen before. All the antibiotics and drugs in the world cannot heal a person. They only alleviate symptoms or destroy infection. Healing is a process of changing lives, getting clean, of attaining balance. The reservation taught me these things.

By the time Whitewolf took me in, I was ripe for help. It took a while, but purification through hundreds of Sweatlodges began to do its good work. While I still have a strong affinity with the Coyote Spirit, I now use the trickster within myself to create stories and teach important lessons rather than manipulate others in service of my ego. That certainly is my aim. Whether or not I am always successful is open to discussion. One dares not be complacent around Coyote.

In the course of my training on the Red Road I learned how to do certain kinds of healing. While I learned to use the Sweatlodge as the place for most of my healing work, I continued to study herbal medicine. There is a Cherokee story of how sickness and medicine came into the world.

In the beginning . . .

all the animals, plants, and human beings lived in harmony and mutual respect. But human beings were selfish. As they grew in numbers they began to treat the animals with callous indifference. They developed weapons and killed without regard to the lives that were taken. The smaller animals, the worms and bugs were smashed without regard. So, the animal nations became so furious that they agreed among themselves that something had to be done to teach the human beings a lesson.

Each group of animals held council and reached a consensus. The deer were first. Anytime a hunter took a deer for food or clothing, he would be required to offer an apology and some corn or tobacco to the spirit of the deceased. If he did not do so, either he or his household would be crippled with arthritis.

The fishes and reptiles agreed to send stomach and intestinal diseases to humans who refused to offer prayers and respect for their catch. Ultimately, all living creatures agreed upon families of diseases that they would inflict upon indifferent humans. Hopefully, human beings would learn something from all this.

The plant nations recognized the justice in what was being proposed, but they also felt the animals were being too harsh. Each plant then volunteered itself as a remedy for specific illnesses. Even weeds had something to offer. Human beings were only required to pay attention and listen with their hearts to the voices of the plants.

So that is how sickness and medicine came into the world.

I love this story. It teaches that health requires us to be in balance with all our relations. Even to use herbs for healing mandates that they be gathered with prayer and respect. There is a season, even a time of day, for each plant to be harvested. When it is being prepared, the plant should be thanked for sharing its gift.

There are three types of healing. The first is herbal and medicinal healing. While I prefer to use herbs when I can, there are times when the powerful intervention of medical drugs is called for. If one has diabetes, the only choice may be to use insulin.

The second type of healing comes from human touch. Parents know the power of touch to soothe a child. Kissing a "boo boo" may stop the pain immediately. "Laying on of hands" is a common form of healing in all the religions. I did it in the Christian ministry years ago. I do it today along with Pipe Ceremony or other Native American healing rituals. Reiki and other Oriental healing systems make use of therapeutic touch.

The important thing for touch healing is the removal of the healer's ego. Grandfather Fools Crow once said that when doing healing, he became a hollow bone through which the healing could flow. It is imperative to remember that the "doctor" is not the one doing the healing. He or she is the transmission line for the life energy, and the body being healed will use that energy in the best way possible.

The third form of healing is spiritual. There are ceremonies in which the Good Spirits of the Creator work miracles. There is no better term for it. Again, Sacred Healing is found in all religions. What a privilege to watch a sick person bound from his or her bed solely as a result of God's grace. Once you see it, you will be changed forever. There are so many ceremonies, so many ways to open the patient to the Creator's power. I have seen healing done with smoke from the Sacred Pipe, with the touch of an eagle-wing fan, with heat from the stones in the Sweatlodge. Usually, the mediation of a medicine man, priest, or spiritual healer is required, but make no mistake about it. The healing flows from God, not man.

I bear witness to the power of healing. I have been helped by herbs, human touch, and the Creator's love, and I am not the same man today that I was 25 years ago.

The Cancer Ballet

1979 – Maryland

My belief in the Sacred Pipe and the power of the Inipi was constantly fed by personal experience. Pain in my upper abdomen drove me to a physician who immediately ordered X-ray studies of my GI tract. Discovering a duodenal ulcer, the doctor outlined his vision of my life for the foreseeable future, a vision I did not share. A doctor is a paid advisor. I expect him to give me his best opinion, to prescribe medication in consultation with me, and to recognize that I will make the medical decisions about my life. This doctor had a paternalistic and condescending attitude which I did not appreciate, so I fired him. I followed the recommendations that made sense to me, drank a lot of antacid, and six months later consulted a new physician.

My new doctor repeated all the diagnostic procedures and set up an interpretation session. I was mildly anxious perched on the stainless steel examining room chair, entertaining myself by studying the anatomical charts, surrounded by the stainless steel trays containing stainless steel needles and stainless steel implements; everything stainless and sterile. Could anyone feel comfortable in one of these suffocating cubby holes?

After an interminable wait, the new doctor strode purposefully through the door, charts in hand, and with a forced smile announced, "There is good news and bad news." He did not offer the choice of which I would hear first. "The good news is that your ulcer is gone. The bad news is that you have a tumor in your small intestine."

My stomach lurched as I calmly inquired, "What do you mean?"

I was trying to absorb this news as he continued, "It would be easier to explain if you saw the X-rays. Let's go downstairs to the radiologist's office."

My mind was reeling. The radiologist escorted us into a darkened room where a series of lighted panels illuminated my X-Rays. The half-light created a surreal atmosphere where two doctors and I danced the dreaded cancer ballet. Their faces, at once animated and serious, underlined the importance of this consult. Both doctors jabbed at the pictures, pointing out the suspected tumor. It was urgent, they insisted, that we schedule a biopsy within the week, "just to be sure."

Outwardly I maintained a professional demeanor, calm, confident, and in charge. Inwardly I was screaming, Hey, wait just a minute here! I need to think about this. I can't schedule this procedure at the drop of a hat just because you say so. My mind rebelled. Aloud, I said, "I want to talk to my consultant first."

"What consultant is that?" My doctor sounded surprised, impatient, skeptical, and offended that I required yet another opinion.

I tried to evade his question by allowing that it was someone I liked to talk with about health matters. But this doctor was not to be eluded, so I finally admitted, "I want to speak to my medicine man."

"Well," he retorted, "you can talk to whomever you like, but these things don't just disappear on their own, and your witch doctor can't heal it. Tell you what," he self-confidently promised, "If your witch doctor cures this, I will send all my patients to him." He smiled at his own fine joke and winked at the radiologist who, being Pakistani, missed the humor.

"Good!" I rejoined mirthfully, "I'll warn him to expect a flood of your patients." The poor radiologist was confused while my doctor forced a pained smile.

Immediately upon returning home, I called Whitewolf and shared my crisis with him.

"Come on out," he said. "We'll ask the Spirits what to do."

Within fifteen minutes I aimed my car toward Whitewolf's camp. The stones were cooking when I arrived and soon we crawled into the sweatlodge. The welcoming heat and steam licked down my bare back, the first comforts in an emotionally dismal day. Entering the Lodge is like being embraced in the consoling arms of the Great Mother.

During the third round Whitewolf asked the Spirits for their direction. I began to chant the Pipe Song while Whitewolf poured enough water on the red hot stones to boil us both. Somewhere beyond the song and intense heat, I heard Whitewolf conversing with the Spirits. I, of course, discerned only his half of the dialogue, "Uh huh. Yes! Sage tea, Uh Huh, three times, Okay. More X-rays." Finally, Whitewolf reported, "Spirits say you are to drink sage tea and pray about this with your Sacred Pipe three times a day for seven days. Then, get X-rayed again. If the growth is gone, that's good. If not, accept the white man's medicine."

I intended to follow the Spirits' directives, hoping to be spared a biopsy and possible cancer treatment. I finally reached the physician by phone, "I will be doing a week of ceremonies for healing. I need you to set up X-rays in seven days to see if the healing worked."

"No," he countered, "I don't want to do that. You shouldn't have so many X-Rays. It isn't necessary."

I was equally adamant that before submitting to exploratory procedures, I would be X-rayed again. He reluctantly complied.

For one week, I assiduously boiled sage tea in the mornings and took it to work. Three times a day I went to a private place outdoors, took out my Sacred Pipe and other ceremonial implements, prayed, and drank the sage tea. Occasionally I remembered the physician's promise to send his patients to Whitewolf if I were cured of the tumor.

I had a stone which came from my first sweatlodge. I had sequestered it in my Bundle, cherishing it as a remembrance of my first Inipi. As I began to pray during the seven days of healing ceremonies, that particular stone caught my attention. I grasped it in my right hand while clasping my Sacred Pipe in the left. The stone calmed and centered me.

Almost imperceptibly the stone began to vibrate in my hand. Each day the quivering grew more pronounced as if it were alive. Later, I learned that my Spirit Teacher had sent the stone as a sacred gift linking me to him.

At the end of seven days I submitted once again to the nasty chalk drink and the X-rays. The technician filled a glass brimming full of the evil brew, handed it to me while wearing a wide, devilish grin, and insisting, "Drink it up, now, quickly and we can see how your insides have changed."

Within minutes, the radiological technician was frowning at the X-Ray. Apprehensively I asked him if he could see the tumor.

Answering, "No," his eyes revealed his puzzlement.

I was barely home before the doctor called. "Duncan, there's a problem. The X-rays didn't pick up your tumor. I want you to be at the hospital in the morning for a special X-ray study."

Ready to have some fun at his expense I retorted, "But I thought you were worried about too much radiation."

"Don't worry about it," he reassured me. "It's no worse than a day in the sunshine."

The following morning at the hospital a radiologist administered a drug which stopped all peristaltic movement in my intestines. With the internal motion stilled, new, more exact pictures were taken. Once again I sweated the results.

Poof! The tumor had vanished.

The doctor advised me to keep close track of my condition. He wanted to do new studies in six months and every six months thereafter. Truth is, he never mentioned my stomach problems again, never offered to X-ray my intestines, and never sent a single patient to Whitewolf. Years later when I had the opportunity to read my medical file, I discovered that the physician had not even included the results of these final studies. The last entry noted that he was waiting for me to set up an appointment for a biopsy. Out of his own need for certainty, he chose to ignore what he failed to understand.

Hospital Feathers

1982 – Southern Maryland

T he voice on the line was urgent, "Sylvia is in the hospital intensive care unit and wants you to come pray for her." It was after 9:00 p.m., but I yanked on my ribbon shirt, grabbed my Sacred Bundle and eagle wing, and headed for our rural, county hospital.

I had no idea how the hospital would receive me in my Native American regalia. My mind went back to my first hospital call as a young pastor. I had come full circle. Back then, I served a church community. Now I was the spiritual leader and Chief of a small Cherokee group. While I would never feel so out of place again as I had during that earlier pastoral visit, this trip would surely be the first of its kind for our local county hospital. Grinning, I couldn't wait to see the facial expressions of the hospital staff.

Entering the lobby, I made my way to the Information Lady who asked quizzically, "How can I help you?" She quickly added, "It's after visiting hours."

"I need directions to the intensive care unit. One of my people, Sylvia Massey, is there and has sent for me."

"Are you family?" She wanted to know.

"No, I'm her minister." What better way could I describe myself in terms the lady would understand? She didn't believe me. The guard sauntered over. He was a large, black man, much taller than myself.

He looked down at me, "What do you want?"

After I explained the situation to his satisfaction, I was directed to Sylvia's private room. Arms full of sacred paraphanelia, I headed down the hallway peripherally aware of startled glances from the nursing staff and perversely delighted by the effect I was creating.

Sylvia was very sick, so weak that she could not raise her head off the pillow. The family had been warned that she was terminally ill. Opening her eyes, Sylvia welcomed me with a wan smile. Before approaching her bed, I checked carefully to be sure that no bottles, tubes or hoses were in harm's way. There would be no field goals during this hospital visit. Not wanting to drain her energy with conversation, I immediately cleansed the room with sage smoke, filled my Sacred Pipe, and began to chant a healing prayer.

At that moment a nurse walked in . . .

It is uncanny how sage smoke smells like marijuana. It sure fooled the nurse because her nostrils flared. Her eyes widened. Right there in front of her, in the sanctity of her hospital, on her own ward, and in her patient's room was this strangely-dressed, long-haired, bandanna-wrapped weirdo with a pipe full of dope.

The nurse drew herself up to full height, took a quick breath, and formed her mouth into a perfect "O." I looked her straight in the eye and said, "Shush, I'm praying". That did it. She backed out of the room, and I finished the ceremony.

I have found that if you are brash enough, you can get away with most anything. If it needs to be done, just do it, and let the world figure it out later. In this case the nurse was so dumbfounded I was finished and gone before anything could happen.

Unlike Sister Jones, Sylvia made a complete recovery.

West

The color is black.

Out of the West come the Wakinyan,
the Thunder Beings, who bring us our dreams,
visions and spiritual growth.
The West is associated with mature
spiritual awareness and sacred teachings.

The following stories carry important teachings
even if housed in humor.

West is represented by
the Horse Nation.

Holy Coyote

Coyote was a dishonest, ego-inflated, bragging, lazy do-nothing prior to the naming ceremony. All the other animals had arrived at sunrise and received their names in due order, but lazy coyote had slept 'til noon. Not only was he the last to arrive at the Creator's lodge, he was hours late.

But Grandfather had a big heart and took pity. He formulated a very special job for Mr. Coyote.

"I am counting on you to live in a good way, to forsake your lying, cunning, selfish behavior." Creator said, "You are now my agent to keep my Creation in balance, and to slay the monsters that prey on my children. You must stay in touch with me every day. I will always be there to help you."

Of course, Coyote danced with elation, crying, "Yes, Grandfather. Thank you. I promise to change my ways and prove myself worthy of Your trust." *It can't be all that hard*, he thought to himself, determined to be a spiritual being.

He left the appointment feeling pretty important, but the animals were laying in wait. They wanted to humiliate and cut him down to size.

Wolf was the first to taunt, "How're you doing, Grizzly? Ready to be the great warrior?"

"Hey, everybody," laughed Badger. "Our great leader just left Grandfather's lodge. Let's gather around, and see how it went."

They pressed around to jeer and taunt him. They called him Grizzly and Eagle and Salmon, all the names he had coveted for himself, but that day Coyote patiently endured their hostility.

Their jeers finally spent, Coyote spoke, "Alright already, I made a damn fool of myself oversleeping. And it was stupid of me to boast and brag about something over which I had no control, but it may interest you to know that the Grandfather assigned me a special role. I am authorized to bring balance when things are out of kilter. I will kill the monsters that torment you. For these projects I am the Grandfather's special Agent."

"No way," they chorused. "Your only job is to be the fool and trouble maker you've always been."

"Not so." Grandfather's voice suddenly thundered over them. "Coyote speaks the truth this time. He is my chosen one. It shall be as he has said."

Cowed, the animals fell into a sullen silence. "How can this be?" They whispered among themselves, but they dared not disrespect the Creator.

"Like I was saying," continued Coyote with a sly grin, "Grandfather has entrusted me with great responsibility. Henceforth, I shall be a new person. I will change my ways. You'll see."

Yeah, sure, all the animals thought.

Mindful of his resolution for righteousness, Coyote returned to his lair to outline his new commission to his wife.

"My love," he said, "I must be off on my rounds, but I will return before sundown with food for you and the children."

"I hope you do," said Mole Woman, "The children went to bed hungry last night, and I won't be able to scavenge enough for them by myself."

"Do not worry, my dear. Your husband has reformed. You and the babies will never be hungry again."

Mole Woman didn't believe him, yet she loved the sound of his tender solicitude. *Maybe he really has changed,* she thought.

Coyote departed on a journey upriver. All morning he visited different villages informing them of his new status. Everywhere he went, he was greeted with hoots of laughter.

He listened patiently to all, then he would reply, "You'll see. I have turned over a new leaf. If you don't believe me, ask Grandfather."

Coyote covered many miles beneath the relentless sun. By early afternoon he was tired and hungry. He remembered his promise to bring food to his children and Mole Woman.

He grumbled to himself, "I am now a great chief with heavy responsibilities. I don't have time to hunt." He remembered his promise to live in a good way, and felt he was doing just that. At that moment, Coyote arrived at a bend in the river where some bears were catching salmon. His growling stomach demanded that he pause. Having no ability as a fisherman, he could only watch ruefully while the bears swiped their huge paws in the water and flipped salmon into their snapping mouths.

One young bear was just learning to fish and was quite clumsy at it. Taking a mighty swing at the water, he caught a large salmon and threw it way over his shoulder where it landed right at Coyote's feet. Snatching up the prize, Coyote bounded behind a boulder and greedily gulped the whole fish, fins and all. He moved so quickly, the young bear did not see the theft. The little fellow searched up and down the beach for his catch. Being both hungry and new at fishing, he had been ecstatic over catching that prize. It should have fallen in plain sight, but it was gone. Dispirited, he turned back to the river to try again, while wily Coyote slid through the bushes and escaped.

Coyote's stunted conscience whispered, *Shame! You stole that fish from a bear child. The least you could have done would be take part of the fish home to your own hungry children.*

But Coyote defended himself. *I'll find something better for them later.* He insisted aloud, "Anyway, Mole Woman must have gathered enough to last them through this day. She won't need my help till later." So, belly full, Coyote continued his journey, searching for tasks to be accomplished and informing all of his new status.

Evening came. *I should check with Creator and tell him what I've been doing,* he thought. Then, remembering how he stole his dinner, Coyote quickly changed his mind. *I'll talk to Grandfather tomorrow,* he decided.

Coming into a village, he called together all the inhabitants and explained to them that he was the newly appointed agent of the Creator. Full of self-importance, Coyote announced, "I am now a Divine Being," but remembering accountability, he hastened to add, "Not Divine in the same way as the Creator, of course, but sort of. I have great magic and powers to balance the Creation and destroy any monsters that harass you."

Maybe it's true, thought the animals of the village. So one by one, each family brought him food until he had enough for a great feast. Having gorged himself, Coyote sat back and invited everyone to share what was left. Only then did he remember his children. It was a remorse that lasted only a moment. *Tomorrow,* he thought, *My family and Creator tomorrow. Tonight, I am just too tired.*

Coyote was not too tired to notice the pretty little female fox that lingered near him drinking in every word however. He noticed how her eyes sparkled with admiration and hero worship. Having never been with a male, she had been saving herself for the perfect mate.

If ever I loved a male, he would have to be like this one, she mused. *Such a fine creature!*

Coyote recognized her vulnerability a mile away. When all but the young fox had returned to their lodges, he spoke, "Would you like to take a walk with me?"

"Oh yes," she gushed.

"Come," he smiled gently, "I will teach you some things."

Billions of stars twinkled overhead as Coyote led her away from the village. The pair sat down to gaze at the gorgeous panoply while Coyote regaled her with legends of the Pleiades and other constellations. The more he talked, the more tightly he wove a spell of seduction around her until she melted into his arms for a night of pleasure.

She thought to herself, *I have found my mate for life.*

Now that was fun, thought wily Coyote. *And tomorrow I will be gone before she misses me.*

Upon awakening the next morning, all set to cuddle again, Miss Fox found herself alone with plenty of time to weep. Coyote had hit the trail, very pleased with himself. He had eaten well, loved well, and slept well. Now a whole new day awaited him.

He trotted at a steady pace by the great river. Before long, a badger ran past him in the opposite direction. Then, a herd of deer nearly ran over him following the badger. A pack of wolves came running at him pell-mell. Raising a hand, he yelled, "Whoa! wait a minute! What's everybody running from?"

The pack chief panted, "There is an evil monster up ahead who is so huge that you can run into his mouth and never realize it. We're getting out of here before he eats us all."

Hmm, thought Coyote. *My kind of a job at last.*

Rummaging around he found a sturdy club, and resumed his journey with purpose. Periodically, groups of refugees would tear past him in mindless panic, while up ahead the road disappeared into a cave.

Ah, he thought. *I'm hot and could use a break. I bet it's cool in there.* So thinking, he plunged into the cave.

The first animal he met was a dying elk.

"Elk woman," he said. "What has happened? You seem to be terribly sick."

"I'm dying and so are you, but you don't know it yet."

"How so?"

"You thought you were entering a cave, but you have entered the mouth of the great giant. Once in here you cannot escape. I am nearly dead from starvation."

Looking around, Coyote saw scores of animals in the same situation. All were starving and dying.

"Fear not," said Coyote. "Your prayers are answered. The Creator has sent me to rescue you."

With one voice they cried, "We don't believe you. You'll die like the rest of us."

"Not at all," said Coyote. "I can't die. I am a very special being. You won't die either; I am here to save you." Pointing to the cave walls, he said, "If we are in the giant's stomach, then the walls of our cave are made of meat and fat. Let's take our knives and carve some."

Cutting a large hunk from the wall, Coyote showed everyone that food was all around them. Immediately, scores of captives were cutting hunks from the giant's insides. The animals were wreathed in smiles, but the giant writhed in pain. He began to jump up and down, holding his stomach. His heart began to pound. Coyote saw it pulsating further down the cave. Taking a long bone from underfoot, he carved a sharp point to make himself a spear.

"I, the Creator's agent, will free you from the giant," he vowed. Taking the spear, he stabbed it repeatedly into the giant's heart. The giant fell over, his great mouth frozen in a silent scream. All the animals escaped, running in panic.

Coyote took his time. Having taken the giant's measure, he felt very proud of himself. Grandfather would be pleased. *

Just wait 'til I tell Mole Woman about this, he thought. *She'll be so proud of me. She'll never hang her head in shame again.* Then he paused, thinking for a moment of his wife and children. *I really ought to go home and make sure they have food.* But that good thought only lasted a moment. *Nah,* he grinned. *I'm on a roll. I'll go tomorrow.*

It was getting on toward sunset. Coyote believed he had something worthwhile to report to the Creator. Sitting down under a shade tree, he cried out, "Creator. Ohhhh Creeaatooor."

There was no response.

He howled a Coyote howl, "Oooowwww, Creeeaaatooor."

There still was no response. Coyote grumbled, "Now where is the Grandfather when you want him?"

Grandfather had settled deep into his recliner chair. Well pleased with the excellence of His creation, He was determined to take a long nap. Just as His eyes were closing, the noise outside disturbed His reverie. In His front yard stood a delegation of earth creatures coughing softly to make their presence known.

"Come in." His voice rumbled like distant thunder.

Terrified, the animal representatives filed into the lodge and stood before Grandfather, heads bowed and shoulders rounded, their submissiveness impeccable.

"What do you want?"

Bear, the acknowledged king of the animals, spoke softly "Grandfather, we know that you are the creator and that we have no right to question your decisions."

"Yes. Go on," Grandfather urged.

"Well, Grandfather, it's about Coyote."

"What about him?" Grandfather demanded to know.

"Grandfather, he lies. He is a braggart. He takes advantage of our women. He steals food from the mouths of our children. He doesn't even take care of his own." Bear looked up from under his eye brows to see how Grandfather was taking this.

"Yes." Grandfather waited.

"Grandfather," Bear continued, "Coyote is the worst sort of creep, but you've made him a special chief. It doesn't seem right to us. Any one of us would be more deserving than him."

Grandfather slumped down in his great chair, closed his eyes, and sank deep into thought. The animals watched in fear and apprehension. As the minutes ticked by, their anxiety mounted.

At last Grandfather opened his eyes. "Of course, you're right," He admitted. "Coyote is everything you claim him to be. But when he came in here at noon rather than sunrise, so excited to get a grand new name, I didn't have the heart to turn him out without some kind of solace."

The animals looked askance at each other, their moods evident from the sourness of their faces.

Grandfather continued, "So I thought long and hard about it. Coyote is Coyote. We all know how his mind works, but he is also brilliant, sometimes. He has courage to match his wiles. I desired a special agent to restore my Creation to balance when needed and to destroy the monsters that plagued my children. I thought, why not use Coyote? Sometimes one will live up to responsibility."

"I don't know, Grandfather. He talks a big line about turning over a new leaf, but he still acts like Coyote. What does he say for himself?" asked Bear.

Grandfather rubbed his chin. "Well, to tell the truth I haven't heard from him, not one word. I told him to check in with me regularly, but he hasn't done so."

"See? That's what we mean. Coyote remains Coyote."

"Okay then," said Grandfather. "Here's what I want you to do. . . ."

Next morning found Coyote lying under a shade tree, ears pricked, eyes scanning the horizon, searching for a situation that needed fixing. His face reflected the disquiet in his soul.

Wonder what happened to Grandfather. I tried and tried to contact him last night and he never answered me. I must be doing something wrong.

Just then deer came trotting up the path.

"There you are, Coyote. I have been sent by the council under authority of Bear. He has called a special meeting and your presence is respectfully requested." Being aware of Coyote's new found status, things had to be stated in a most politically correct way.

"Hum. Ah. Well, I have many responsibilities," Coyote demurred. "One never knows where the next monster will appear or the next dis-balance manifest itself."

"Bear says it's very important, sir."

"Oh, All right. I'll come."

Soon Coyote found himself at the center of the animal Council.

Bear spoke, "Ahem. Coyote, we have called you here with the unanimous consent of all the animals, and we even have permission from Grandfather, Himself."

Coyote's pricked his ears. This sounded ominous.

"We admit that we were quite dubious upon hearing of your appointment as the Creator's special agent. You realize, I'm sure, that we doubted your ability to behave honorably, and I must say that you have not disappointed us. I hasten to add, however, that we are appreciative for your destroying the evil giant. You also tried hard to straighten out a whole community of animals who couldn't keep their identities straight even if you did mock them with sacred stoppers."

All the animals had snickered at the foolish creatures with their corn cobs and crystals.

Bear continued, "We have decided to help you live up to your calling. Grandfather wants you to succeed, and so do we."

"I don't need your help, thank you. I can do it myself," groused Coyote. He thought, *Who do these miserable creatures think they are, offering to help me?*

Bear spoke again, "Grandfather wants to know why you haven't checked in with Him."

"It's His fault. I tried last night. I called and called, but He didn't answer me."

"Maybe you can't get outside your big ego enough to listen for Him."

"What is that supposed to mean?" Coyote growled.

Rattlesnake, who was recognized as a very spiritual being, lay in a relaxed coil beside bear. He hissed, "Trouble with you is, you don't pay attention. You've got to stop your incessant talking, move into the silence, and use the ears of your heart."

"I still don't understand," grumbled Coyote.

"Your head is chocked full of worry that we won't see how important you are. You invent elaborate games and schemes to impress us." Rattlesnake paused to let his words sink in. "If Grandfather has chosen you, that's enough for us to at least give you a chance to prove yourself. Forget trying to impress us. Go out into the desert, sit down and relax. Speak simply to Grandfather. Let your mind be still and your heart open. You may learn something."

"It's that simple, huh?"

"Sometimes the most profound things are the most simple," assured Rattlesnake.

That evening Coyote returned to Mole Woman and the children. In his arms he carried several quail he had caught. There was great happiness in the lodge as he regaled his family with stories of his exploits, but some things he kept to himself.

Before retiring for the night, he slipped out into the desert to speak with Grandfather. He let his mind grow quiet. He stifled his need to boast or day-dream of his greatness. Quietly he cried, "Hau, Grandfather. This is your grandson, Coyote. Thank you for this wonderful day. Please speak to me."

In His lodge the Creator heard Coyote's soft prayer. His heart filled with joy. "Coyote, my son, it is good to hear your voice."

Startled, Coyote jumped to his feet. Grandfather's words surrounded him in the clear desert air. Coyote took a deep breath and settled down to listen. As he did, Grandfather's words brought him great inner peace.

The Creator continued, "You have made a good start. You have done some good work, but you have also misused your powers. Try harder. In all that you do, show respect for my children. What good is it to kill giants if you hurt or take advantage of My innocent children, and even your own family?"

Coyote knew what the Creator meant. He cried, "Hau, Grandfather. I shall try harder."

The next morning, Coyote began his rounds again. This time he was aware that the animals were pulling for him. He also knew they were watching him.

Eagle swooped down and landed in a nearby tree. "Hau! Coyote!"

Coyote said, "Yes. What do you want?"

"There is a Stone Monster killing many people in the Big Bend country."

"I'm on my way," said Coyote.

As he turned to go, he spied a beautiful, young female bathing in the river.

"Ah," he said. "I'll go in a little while."

Eagle replied, "No. Go NOW."

"You're right," agreed Coyote with some ambivalence. He turned toward the Big Bend country, but he kept one eye turned toward the maiden.

Day by day Coyote struggled to balance the world and fulfill his commission, and day by day Coyote fought to control his ego and appetites. Each night found him meditating in the desert, listening to the music of Grandfather's words and the resonances of the Creation.

As time passed his spiritual powers grew, but so did his temptations. The two go hand in hand.

And so Coyote remains Coyote to this day.

---

* The story of Coyote and the Giant is told in different forms by several North Western Tribes. I have taken the liberty of re-shaping it and including it within a larger story of my own making.

Vision Quest

I stand
> Toward the sundown place,
Silent
> Before the endless hunger.
Wakan Tanka
> See my tears
> > Like ice
> > Soothing the hot regret
Of lost years.
Let angels carry my spirit
> To that distant holy place
> > Of Vision.
Let me be touched by ancestors
> Long past
> > Ever present,
Standing with me
> Toward the sundown place.

—Sings-Alone

Facing West: The Fourth Vision Quest; Already a Fool

T he spade punched its way into the baked and rocky soil. Bit by bit the hole deepened until it was deep and wide enough for my purposes. Sometimes digging a hole must precede climbing a mountain. Such is the case for longer Vision Quests. All parts of the body from brains to bowels participate in a four day/four night Hanblecheya.

Forcing a smile at my crude humor, I looked behind me at my altar, prepared and ready for the ordeal. My personal performance during previous Hanblecheyas had fallen a mile short of spectacular. Somehow, I had managed to arrive at the end of the four-year, Vision Quest cycle. Only under the most rare circumstances would one attempt Hanblecheya without food or water, naked, and exposed to the elements for more than four days and nights.

My mind rebelled at the foolishness of this undertaking. My heart, though frightened, was determined to see it through. So, I finished digging my latrine, checked around the area making sure that everything was in place, and returned to the community for the final preparations, the last meal, and the sweatlodge.

Sunset found me in my altar, once again praying for pity and endurance. The Hanblecheya began on Wednesday afternoon. Friday sunrise found me still watching, praying, waiting. It was a very quiet time, but then again, I had nothing but time. So far, there were no Visions, Dreams, or Visitations.

Later in the morning a mockingbird perched on one of my altar poles, a large sprig of sage dangling from its bill. It watched me intently for a few moments, then dropped the sage and flew away. Back home in Southern Maryland the mockingbird had joined me every morning to sing up the sunrise. Taking position in the bush next to me he would trill his heart out. Now he was participating in my Vision Quest by offering me sacred sage! Gratefully, I stuck the sage in a quilled prayer wheel and bequeathed it to my sacred bundle.

The atmosphere around the altar filled with expectancy as if the mockingbird portended things to come. Nothing specific occurred the rest of the day, but there was a tightness in the air, a pressure beginning to build. Up to this point I had suffered very little. I was dehydrated as one might expect in a Vision Quest, but my thirst was manageable. The June temperature was unnaturally cool. Even the elements had pity on me. Vision Questing often feels like 95% tedium and 5% action, and if tedium dulls the senses, one could miss the 5% when it happens. I struggled hard to stay focused, to be alert for whatever might come.

Deep in the night I prayed, "Grandfather, one thing I desire from my Hanblecheya. For three years I have worn this special stone around my neck. I was told that it is my Stoneman. The Spirits even disclosed his name, Trail Keeper, but I know nothing of him. I want to know my Spirit Teacher. Hau, Mitakuye Oyas'in."

"Well, what do you want to know?" Behind me a voice spoke. My first impulse was to throw the Pipe over my head and run.

Getting a grip on myself, I stammered, "Grandfather, I would like to see you."

A face floated in the air in front of me, an old face, full of amusement, the visage of a Plains Indian. "How's that?" he replied, smiling.

"Grandfather, I would like to see all of you."

Immediately, an elderly Indian dressed in an old plaid shirt and blue jeans materialized in front of me and slowly pirouetted, his face split in a mischievous grin. "Okay, how's that?"

"Thank you, Grandfather," I whispered, subdued.

Trail Keeper sat down beside me and was silent for what seemed an eternity. My heart was pounding but I dared not speak. He looked straight ahead pensively, in no hurry. I held my Pipe tightly, forgetting that I should offer it to him. I was too thunderstruck to do anything but hunker down respectfully.

Finally turning toward me, Trail Keeper asked, "Well, Grandson, what do you want to know?"

"Grandfather, could you tell me about yourself? Who are you?"

"I lived on this earth many years ago, when the first white men invaded our territory. I was heyoka and what you would call a medicine man. You don't need to know anything more about me. Nothing else matters except that I chose to work with you."

"But why me, Grandfather?"

"Because you were already a fool," he replied.

It took a while to absorb that. I was known in the community as a clown, making people laugh even in ceremony. But I wasn't sure what Trail Keeper meant.

"Had you never wondered," he continued, "what happened to you last year on that lightning-swept hill? Didn't it seem strange that right in the middle of a violent storm you went to sleep and didn't wake up until the Wakinyan had passed?"

Actually, I hadn't thought much about it.

"Last year you were made heyoka by the Thunder Beings. I chose to be your teacher years ago. You received your Stoneman as a link between then and now. Last year's Hanblecheya formalized the path you will walk the rest of your life."

The teachings continued. He instructed me in certain ways of healing; where and how to position the patient, specific kinds of ceremony. He gifted me a healing song, and while laughing, teased me, "It has to be a simple song or you couldn't learn it." Then he was gone. My altar rocked the rest of the night. Spirits and medicine helpers crowded around. The mockingbird suffused the darkness with songs. What a night!

After sunrise I slept, exhausted and weak. During the remaining daylight hours, I thought about Trail Keeper, rehearsed his teachings, and committed them to memory.

Far into my fourth night, I waited, excited and alert, hoping he would visit again. Without warning, I was poised at a cave opening. A dim light emanated from inside. A worn path led inward, but I was uncertain whether or not to follow it. I debated with myself, "They must have put me here for a purpose. It won't do me any good to hang around the entrance and worry about it." So, taking a deep breath, I lunged ahead. After twenty-five or thirty yards the path disappeared under debris where the right side of the cave had collapsed. Was this a sign to stop? I hesitated.

Trail Keeper emerged from the shadows, took my hand, and said, "Come on." He helped me clamber over the boulders until we reached a path on the other side. As my guide, he led the way.

"Look down there," he said, pointing to the left of the path. Strange pits were interspersed along the floor. They seemed to be pulsating, opening and closing, like sucking lips.

"Those are the mouths of the people. Watch out for them. If your ego grows so bloated that you believe you can meet everyone's needs, you will be lured from the path and you will die."

"Look up there to the right," he continued. "See the ugly green light shimmering behind the debris? That light represents evil. Power can be used for evil or for good, but if you perform evil, you will lose your path and die. Beware of the temptation to use evil for good purposes." He was warning me in advance that old Coyote can corrupt us before we realize we have been conned. We may be tricked to believe we are everybody's salvation, or that we are free to do anything for a just cause. Psychologists describe it as the seduction of the ego and the lust for power. I think Trail Keeper would have simply called it "being human."

The cave passage opened into a larger room. In the center of the room burned a small fire around which six older men sat cross-legged. One of them had a stiff knee from an old injury. He resembled the actor, Lee Marvin, with a Mohawk hair cut. Telling me to wait, Trail Keeper approached the group. An animated conversation ensued. Obviously talking about me, They kept looking in my direction but gave me no invitation to join Them.

After a bit, Trail Keeper came back to me and reported, "These are your six Grandfathers. They will not talk with you because you don't yet know how to listen. They will coach me and I will work with you. Later, when you get your ears open, They will join me in speaking directly with you."

Suddenly, I was back in my altar on the hill, alone.

The sounds of drumming and singing echoed from beyond the hill. Listening intently, I failed to recognize the song. Then, Trail Keeper appeared and sat beside me once again.

"Hello, Grandfather. Thank you for that Vision. It gives me a lot to think about," I said.

"Good," he replied. "Now here is a song for you to sing at the beginning of any ceremony. It is your own Spirit-calling song. It will summon me, your medicine helpers, and other Good Spirits nearby, and let us know that you need our help when you are about to do something important. This is not for everyone to sing. This is yours alone." True to his previous word, it was a simple song that even I could learn. I repeated it again and again until the song was imprinted on my mind.

Trail Keeper disappeared and I sensed that the Vision Quest was finished. The altar was quiet and my heart mirrored the stillness. "Grandfather, Wakan Tanka, if my Hanblecheya is finished please give me a sign." Immediately, the night's stillness was shattered by Elvis proclaiming "You ain't nothing but a hound dog." Teenagers were partying beyond the ridge. It was time to go home. Later, I learned that no one else had heard the racket.

As I stumbled down the hill, weak and dizzy from my ordeal, my Medicine Helpers supported me. Upon seeing my teacher, I cried, "Whitewolf, either I have had an amazing experience or I am certifiably crazy."

Some may still wonder.

Coyote Speaks

1939 – Rural Kentucky

I n one of my earliest memories, I am very small, maybe four years old. Next to me lying flat in the grass is my cousin, Patti, two years older than I and infinitely more sophisticated. We are hiding in the shadows behind a circle of chairs in which our relatives sit telling stories. We must be very quiet; one small squeak and they will pack us off to bed.

I remember Grandpa telling of his wagon trip west when he was a lad. His family was attacked by Pawnee on those rolling plains. He escaped by jumping into an empty barrel, rolling off the wagon and down a hill. From a gulch behind a scrawny old tree, he watched the Pawnee try to destroy the wagon. "Don't make 'em like those any more," he would say. "Dammed Pawnee couldn't tear up that wagon, or even burn it, no matter how hard they tried."

The story of that barrel and the wagon were etched into my young memory.

"Yep, those old wagons were somethin' else." my Grandpa continued. "Daddy used his to haul wood. Went out one day to cut his-self a load. He was meandering down near the creek bottom when here came an ol' hoop snake. You know about them? Well, they take their tail in their mouths, and roll to where they're goin'. When they get close to their mark they straighten out like an arrow and shoot tail first into the prey. Deadly poisonous those snakes. Poison's in their tail barb. One sting and you're a gonner for sure."

Wide-eyed, I looked over at Patti. She covered her mouth and with her pointer finger shushed me into silence.

"Well, Daddy looked up just in time to see that ol' snake straighten out for the kill. He was aiming for the mule's flank. Daddy popped that mule with the whip. The mule jumped forward and the snake slammed into the wagon tongue. Daddy said it was a real sight. That snake hit so hard it got stuck. It was a writhing around tryin' to pull loose but couldn't. Daddy took the ax and killed it, but the poison had started doin' its work on that wagon tongue. The tongue began to swell until the wagon couldn't move. Daddy started to pare it down with his ol' ax. The more he cut, the more it swole until finally he had a whole wagon load of wood and the tongue was back to normal. Those old wagons was somethin' else."

Now, it is my turn to sit around the fire and tell stories. I am the grandfather; story teller to a new generation of listeners. Hopefully, they will memorize our legends and history, and if they are wise, they will learn from my trickster tales how to live good and respectful lives. If they are lucky, they will also know to be aware of Ol' Coyote.

The Shaman's Helmet

1983 – Good Medicine Gather, Old Joe, Arkansas

Many Native Americans feel sorry for the dominant culture which, for the most part, has forgotten the magic of story-telling. Television and movies are fine, but nothing can replace the spell spun between teller and audience;

One night at a Good Medicine Gathering, as a fire played lights and shadows over up-turned listening faces and a breeze from Arkansas's White River washed them with gentle coolness, my audience hunkered down by the fire waiting once again to become children under the story-teller's spell. I had finished a Coyote tale and called, "Let's hear Chief White Feather."

"Oh, yes!" Everyone loved Chief White Feather's tales.

White Feather was a master. His formidable figure emerged from the shadows. Stepping in front of the fire, he planted his feet widely apart and held his staff far out to the side. White Feather stood some 5'8" tall, weighing about 300 pounds, with snow white hair, round flushed face, and blue sparkling eyes that miss nothing; a modern Moses on Mt. Sinai, except for his head piece.

Parked on White Feather's hoary head was a bleached cow pelvis. The pelvic bones swept down the sides of his face, and on the front were glued two cow horns. His helmet was vaguely reminiscent of a Samurai warrior's head piece.

I don't remember the stories he told, but White Feather in his cow pelvis made an indelible imprint on my mind. Throughout the following year I periodically reflected on that helmet. White Feather in a cow's pelvis inspired me to create a coyote teaching tale. When the Good Medicine Society next met, I was ready.

Please understand that teaching in the Coyote way is part of my medicine. I abhor the charlatans who promulgate all manner of tripe in the name of Indian spirituality. The young people and adults who attend these gatherings want to absorb real Indian spirituality and practices. They are committed to recapturing the ways of their ancestors.

Part of learning this path is to carefully weigh what one hears. Otherwise, our students could fall prey to swindlers who sell nonsense in the name of Native American religion. Our young people must never believe an instruction until it is tested by common sense and judged consistent with what they have previously learned.

At the next gathering, I had hardly parked my truck, when a group of eager young adults crowded around to visit with Grandfather Sings-Alone. We exchanged a few pleasantries and then I began my plan, "You know, I have been thinking all year about Chief White Feather and his cow pelvis helmet," I said.

"Yeah," they remembered.

"I found a library book, *Spiritual Practices Of The Plains Indians From 1730 to 1850*, and researched it." They were hooked.

"The book said that medicine men, indeed, would wear buffalo pelvises on their heads. That kind of surprised me because I had never seen pictures of it." I paused for dramatic effect.

"But even more surprising was the fact that a young person studying medicine ways would take a buffalo vagina, stretch it over his or her head, and let it dry into a perfectly fitting, rawhide apprentice's cap."

Their responses were somewhere between a reverent "Wow!" and a startled "What?" I pressed on, "This helped them move between the worlds, like being born back and forth, learning to make the transition from this dimension to the next. They would wear these vagina helmets until they could move in and out of alternate realities with ease. Afterwards, they would graduate to the full buffalo pelvis, shaman's helmet."

It took a moment for the import of this teaching to sink in. When I saw they had it, I continued, "It would seem to me that if you are serious about learning medicine ways, you need to make yourselves vagina medicine caps. You know that you aren't likely to find a dead buffalo, but you can go to a packing house and get all the cow vaginas you need."

After another theatrical moment I added, "Listen, I need to go set up my camp. We'll talk later." I exited before the serious expression on my face collapsed.

"Duncan, are you going to leave them like that?" Priscilla whispered urgently in my ear, "They might really believe you."

"Yep, and if they do, they deserve a trip to the packing house."

We were both laughing as I added, "Can you imagine what the guys at the packing house will think when these kids arrive demanding a bunch of cow privates?

Tatanka Wee Wee

1989 – Sings-Alone's Place, Southern, Maryland

Coyote has an eye for the unwary sophisticate. He grinned as he watched the greenhorn try to light a sacred fire the "right" way in the rain. Human beings are foolishly serious when their pride is on the line. She struck one match after the other, prayerfully, earnestly, desperately trying to coax fire from wet kindling.

"Would ya like a little paper in there?" Coyote spoke sotto voce.

"No," she grumbled, "Give me a little time here."

More semi-dry leaves and tinder were added and more matches sacrificed. Members of the community stood by and watched with interest. She was determined to do it the right way.

"You know, I have seen many a Sioux use gasoline to start a fire in the rain." Coyote was being helpful. "I remember a Lakota guy throwing a pint of gasoline into the fire and blowing the whole thing apart. Almost incinerated the sweatlodge."

She didn't bother to look up. Her fingers fumbled with yet another match. Several of the onlookers brought a few more leaves and damp twigs which were officiously tucked in among the larger sticks.

Coyote wouldn't quit. "You don't have to struggle so hard. Do it the right way, but if the fire won't burn, you may have to help it along. There's some charcoal lighter in the barn."

"No! This fire is going to burn!" she snapped.

More matches. A feeble wisp of smoke, then nothing.

Loose strands of hair were falling in her eyes. Pushing them back distractedly, she looked around for something "appropriate" that would be dry enough to burn.

"If you're looking for dry paper, I can get some from the house." Coyote, the epitome of helpfulness and concern, bent over her, following her every futile attempt to coax fire from wet wood. Half-smothered chuckles escaped from a few observers who vicariously enjoyed Coyote's "helpfulness". One never uses paper to start a Sacred Fire.

Her eyes were laser beams of hostility. "I can do this, and I will do it right."

"The right way is to do what will make the fire burn." Coyote was being so patient. "In the old days the Lakota kept an old Tatanka (bull buffalo) tied outside the camp. When they needed to start a sweatlodge fire with wet kindling, they would lead the old bull over to the fire. He would lift his leg and pee on the fire. Buffalo piss is just like kerosene."

"Their name for the old fella was Tatanka Wee Wee," he added.

Doubt and determination struggled with the desire to believe. Her eyes momentarily softened as she turned to face her tormentor.

He pressed the point, "What you want is a natural substance to start the fire. Since you don't have any buffalo pee, use natural kerosene or charcoal lighter. It is all from the Grandmother." Coyote was grinning, "Remember ol' Tatanka Wee Wee."

She looked at the others for confirmation of his buffalo piss story. Several women of the camp stood there, arms folded, minding their own business, but shaking their heads ever so slightly.

Grimly stubborn, she hunkered down once again with her matches.

Coyote turned away, kicking the dirt as he walked to the house.

Grandfather, I Am Going to Drink

1981 – My honeymoon with Priscilla

"If you carry the Pipe for the people, you must give up booze." Whitewolf was absolutely clear about the responsibilities of a Pipe Carrier. "You must be ready to fill your Sacred Pipe and pray whenever it is needed. You cannot touch your Pipe to your lips if you have had alcohol or drugs that same day. Drinking liquor and carrying the Pipe are mutually exclusive."

Alcohol has scourged the Indian Nations, destroying lives and families. To drink liquor and smoke the Sacred Pipe on the same day would be disrespectful to the point of sacrilege. But Whitewolf recognized that Priscilla and I liked to drink. It was a part of her Irish heritage that I heartily endorsed. Careful to drink sparingly, we nevertheless enjoyed it when we did.

I quit. The medicine bag on my belt reminded me daily that I walked a sacred road. The Chanunpa Wakan demanded an awesome commitment, and I would not jeopardize my role as a Pipe carrier by drinking.

When Priscilla and I married, we began our honeymoon in New Orleans and proceeded to New Mexico and Arizona visiting the Pueblos. On our tour of the Pueblos and the Navaho Reservation, we would not be personal guests of any Indians, so we planned to ignore the drinking ban. I saw no reason for abstinence since no one could expect me to do ceremony. I faced the Creator at sunrise and explained, "Ho, Tunkasila Wakan Tanka, my woman and I have just married and are going on our honeymoon. We want to have fun. Grandfather, I stand before you as a two-legged and tell you that I intend to drink. I will not drink with Indian people. I will do harm to no one, but my woman and I will drink and have fun together."

Sometimes, a man must take responsibility for himself and inform the Creator of his intentions.

So we toasted New Orleans, Albuquerque, Santa Fe and all points in between. We honeymooned and played full time and ignored Whitewolf's prohibitions on liquor. My drinking hurt no one. Upon returning to Maryland, our jobs, and our Indian community, I remembered how harmlessly I enjoyed booze and decided to continue drinking but would "check it out" with the Creator.

Once again I confronted the Grandfather, "Ho, Tunkasila Wakan Tanka, my woman and I enjoyed our honeymoon. We drank some, but we did not drink with Indians or around the Pipe. I see no harm in continuing to drink the same way. Grandfather, I intend to use alcohol unless you show me a clear sign otherwise." There exists no fool like a self-deluding fool. In the meantime, I blissfully forgot that I had asked for a sign.

Snow covered the ground as we drove to work that first morning. By afternoon a few more inches had fallen. The roads were a mess by the time we returned home in the evening. That night when I disrobed for bed, no medicine bag dangled from my belt! I had worn that medicine bag for years. Two buck skin thongs secured it. If one broke, the other would hold it safe until the bag could be repaired. It had hung two pant loops back on my belt so that if the belt opened the medicine bag would remain safe.

I thoroughly searched the house. The bag had disappeared. Driving slowly through the snow, I returned to the office and rummaged everywhere for it. My stomach locked into knots. My mind whirled with visions of divine retribution. This bag and I had been inseparable for years.

Back home, I filled my Pipe and begged, "Grandfather, I hear you. No more drinking! Please, Grandfather, give me back my medicine bag." A pitiful man slept in my bed that night.

By the next morning despair over the loss of my medicine pouch had settled like a gloom over me. My conscience accused me of unfaithfulness. After choking down my breakfast in anguish, I started for work. Priscilla drove, negotiating the snow on our divided, four-lane highway.

Suddenly, looming bigger than life, right in the middle of our highway lane, lay my medicine bag.

"Stop! there it is," I shouted.

"What?" Priscilla looked at me quizzically.

"My medicine bag. You just ran over it." Priscilla coaxed the car to the highway apron. I raced back to retrieve the bag. It was not wet from the snow. It had not been smashed by any of the hundreds of cars on the highway. As the loops were unbroken; the bag had obviously not been yanked off my belt. My medicine bag was intact and it had come home. Gratefully, I slid it onto my belt where it belonged. I got the sign I had prayed for.

Indians Can't Be Hypnotized

1980 – Whitewolf's place

Grandfather Eli, founder of the Good Medicine Society, taught, "Whatever is true is true in all times and in all places."

I spent a lot of my available time at Whitewolf's Camp in dogged pursuit of my roots, absorbing all I could of the spiritual teachings. During my working hours I taught classes in Clinical Psychology at a nearby University and provided psychotherapy in my private practice.

A couple of interesting parallels began to emerge as I considered the relationships between the healing work of psychologists and the healing ceremonies of Native American practitioners. As I listened to Whitewolf in the sweatlodge communicate with the Spirits, he seemed to enter a trance state. In both my work and private life I used trances to facilitate entry into altered states of consciousness.

Trained in hypnosis, I could not help but compare it with the medicine man's altered state of consciousness. It also seemed to me that Transcendental Meditation and other meditative practices shared the same characteristics. It occurred to me that perhaps all of us were using the same processes to transport our minds into alternate realms of reality. I ran the idea by Whitewolf. His reply was short and direct, "No real Indian can be hypnotized!" It was one of those pronouncements about which any argument would have been a waste of time.

Staying at Whitewolf's place was my old friend Colquit. He was strongly attracted to Native American spiritual practices so it was natural for him to follow me to Maryland and Whitewolf's camp.

One afternoon, as several of us tended the sweatlodge fire, Colquit was some distance away experimenting with black powder used in muzzle loading rifles. Colquit figured that black powder would fire more slowly than regular gun powder. Mounding up a small pile of black powder, he tried to set it off, and when it did not flash, he bent over it to see what went wrong.

At that instant, the powder blew. Colquit flew backwards. We saw him collapse but had no idea what had happened. We ran toward him, and as we got closer, we saw that his face had transformed into a grotesque mask. Squinting reflexively at the explosion saved his eyes. Only the skin in the creases of his frown kept its natural color. His exposed skin was burned, leaving his face in a weird pattern of black and pink.

We helped him to the house where the women stretched him out on the living room floor and bathed his face in cold water. Colquit was suffering but did not want to go to the emergency room. Cold water was the best available treatment. As the women were adequately caring for him, the men proceeded to the sweatlodge.

Later that evening, after the Inipi ceremony, the living room was crammed with exhausted Indians. Colquit moaned, "Duncan, I hurt bad. Could you hypnotize me and take some of this pain away?" Colquit knew of my hypnosis training.

"Sure," I replied, with more confidence than I felt. Actually, I was a little worried about Whitewolf who was watching with a mixture of curiosity and disapproval. I had always been careful to keep my professional business far away from the camp. Recognizing my own ignorance about Indian spirituality, I was there to learn, not to show off. My friend, however, needed help. So, I began the hypnotic induction, suggesting that he breathe deeply and begin to let his body relax and move out of conscious awareness. I guided him into trance with visualizations of cool waters and gentle breezes wafting over his face. Finally, as the nerve endings relaxed and the pain subsided, Colquit closed his eyes and rested peacefully.

Staying focused on Colquit's breathing pattern, I forgot the others in the room. Finally, as he slipped into trance, I took a moment to look up. Whitewolf's chin rested on his chest. Eyes closed, he was far into the other world. All around the room, Indian brothers and sisters slumped in their chairs, relaxed, limp, breathing deeply, and in that altered state of reality with which they had become familiar in the sweatlodge and other ceremonies. This time, instead of being assisted by intense heat, darkness, drumming and song, they had entered by an hypnotic path.

Coyote grinned. "Indians can too be hypnotized!" He said softly, not to awaken anyone in the room.

The Sacred Pipe

Even though the Colorado River Indian Tribes—the Mohaves, Chemehuevies, Navaho, and Hopi—did not traditionally use the Sacred Pipe, I had wanted one. I had desired a Pipe from the time I first met Rolling Thunder, and that hunger grew within me after I came to live on the reservation. From the time I first arrived, the Pipe pressed itself on my awareness. Standing each morning in the desert facing East, I would wait for the sun to crest the distant mountains. The reservation was bounded by small mountains running north and south on its flanks. I could track the rising sun by the shadows sliding down the western slopes behind me. At the exact moment of sunrise, following Rolling Thunder's example, I would offer tobacco to the rising Sun or prayerfully smoke tobacco in a corn cob pipe.

I searched for my Sacred Pipe in Phoenix and Tucson, ignorant of the fact that a Pipe could be ordered from Pipestone, Minnesota. Visiting all the Indian stores, I found many stone pipes, but none of them spoke to me. One afternoon in Phoenix I saw an antique shop. I usually ignored such stores, but this time I felt compelled to enter. Casually exploring among the shelves, my eyes lit on a dusty Indian pipe. Bowl and stem joined, lonely, surrounded by Anglo junk, it bore mute testimony to the sacred Red Road. Without hesitation I knew this was my Pipe. With joy and relief, I turned it over and inspected it from all angles. I claimed it as my own.

In the beginning, I had no idea how to handle the Pipe in a sacred way and knew nothing of the protections it required. Ignorant as I was, I honored my Chanunpa and made prayers through it. It would be two years before I would learn the ways of the Sacred Pipe, and three years before I would evolve into a Pipe Carrier.

In my ignorance and haste, I made all the mistakes Whites and Anglo-assimilated Indians typically make in approaching this sacred road. Wanting to be instant shamans, they demand "how to" books for complex ceremonies. Hungry for spiritual grounding, they gulp and choke on spiritual practices that require years of preparation. In too big a hurry, I mishandled the Pipe. I did not know how to fill it, offer it, pray with it appropriately, or physically protect it. I did not intentionally violate the customs of respect. I played Pipe carrier without taking time to become one.

Fortunately, the Creator is not interested in punishing us for being human. Wallowing in guilt is a useless indulgence. One must seek out a right way, correct his mistakes, and plunge ahead into life. Coyote's lessons are painful and embarrassing, but we learn from them. He has no joy in afflicting us with permanent self-recriminations.

When I linked-up with Whitewolf, I began to learn the proper ways of keeping a Pipe. My intent to honor and pray with the Pipe had been clear from the beginning. Finally, I learned to do it in the right way.

When I take that red-stone Pipe bowl in my left hand, I think of our people. It is their color. That bowl is the heart of the Indian Nations, held in my left hand because it is the hand closest to my heart. That bowl, being made from rock, also represents the Grandmother earth. It is feminine.

The stem is made from a tree; quite often, the sumac tree. The stem will usually be decorated with buckskin and eagle feathers. The stem represents the animal and plant worlds. It is masculine. Inserting the stem into the bowl, you have joined the masculine and feminine, and you have what our children call animal, vegetable and mineral. Holding the Pipe, I always think of the Negro spiritual, *He's Got The Whole World In His Hands*. That is exactly what I feel.

My little Sacred Pipe is directly related to the Buffalo Calf Pipe which came to the Lakota people nineteen generations ago. That original Pipe still resides on the Cheyene River Reservation and is protected by Grandfather Arvol Looking Horse, the 19th Generation Pipe Keeper. The name of every Pipe Keeper from the beginning is known to the people.

That first Chanunpa Wakan may be the most sacred item in this world. What other religion has any thing to compare to it; given by the Holy Ones, and kept in a known lineage from the beginning? Here is the story of how the first Sacred Pipe came to the Lakota.

The Story of the White Buffalo Calf Pipe

Many years ago, long before the White Man invaded this land, the people lived together in respect and harmony. The elders and orphans were protected and fed by the stronger members of the tribe. Everyone looked out for each other and contributed to the well being of all.

Then a bad spirit insinuated itself into the consciousness of the people. Hunters began to hog the best parts of the kill for themselves. The old people and the orphans knew hunger for the first time while others in the villages filled their bellies with game. The ancient teachings of generosity and respect were forgotten. A cloud settled over the Lakota.

The Winters were long, and even though the people put food away for the cold months, there was always hunger in the early Spring until the animals reappeared and the hunts could resume. It so happened one year, that Spring arrived but the animals did not. Bellies were swollen in starvation. The weaker among the people died.

Each day the young men would search everywhere for game, but they seldom found even a rabbit.

One morning two brothers went out to hunt. We do not know if they were blood brothers or kola (the deepest kind of friendship) brothers. It doesn't matter. All morning they hunted but found nothing. Finally, creeping low to the ground, they reached a hill crest. Lying flat, their eyes searched for any movement in the valley below or the hillside across from them. They were about to give up when they noticed movement. Something was making its way down the hill. It was a woman. As she drew closer, they saw that she was dressed in white buckskin. She had a regal carriage, moving with grace through the grasses.

One of the brothers had an evil thought. He said, "There is a woman over there, and she does not have a man to protect her. I'm going to take her."

His brother replied, "You'd better leave her alone. She may be Wakan (Sacred)."

"Nonsense." And with that, the bad brother slipped down the hill and approached the woman. When he was directly in front of her. They were enveloped in a cloud. Then, as the cloud dissipated, only the woman stood there. At her feet was a skeleton. The old people say that snakes and all manner of unclean things were crawling through the bones.

The woman looked up at the brother who was watching wide-eyed and signaled him to come down. Of course, the remaining brother was terrified, but he obeyed the Wakan woman.

When he was close to her, she said, "Go back to your chief, Standing Hollow Horn, and tell him that I will come soon. I have something for the people."

The brother ran all the way back to the village and breathless told everything he had seen and heard. The chief ordered a large council tipi to be erected. Soon, as She promised, the Wakan Woman walked into the village and entered the tipi. The Chiefs and headmen followed behind her, and the people crowded around outside so that all could hear.

For several days She stayed with them. She spoke with sadness over the way the people had forgotten what it meant to be human beings. She reminded them that only love and generosity would keep the tribe alive. Then, She gave the Lakota their seven Sacred Rites. Finally, just before She left, the Wakan Woman opened a special bundle. Lifting up the Bowl and Stem, She presented Chief Standing Hollow Horn the very first Chanunpa Wakan. She taught the people how to use and protect this Pipe, and She told them that as long as the people lived in respect and harmony, remembering the teachings of their grandfathers and Grandfather above, this Pipe would protect them. Whatever they needed would come to them.

When She finished, She walked out of the Tipi toward the prairie. The people followed at a respectful distance. They watched as She was enveloped in a cloud. When this cloud drifted away, a white buffalo calf was rolling in the dirt. Jumping up, It trotted off over the hill. To this day, the Wakan Woman is called the White Buffalo Calf Maiden. Whenever we smoke our Sacred Pipes, we remember that She brought the Pipe to us as a gift from the Powers above.

That Holy Pipe reformed my life. I love and honor it to this day.

Mom's Lowanpi

1980 – Whitewolf's place

Priscilla's mother earned an M.D. degree from Johns Hopkins Medical School in the 1920's when women were not freely welcomed into medicine. Everyone loved her. She had an inquiring mind which was never encapsulated by her degree. She loved anthropology, archeology, the theater, and literature. Her husband, Dave, garnered international fame as the father of neuro-ophthalmology.

So, in 1980, when Priscilla introduced me to the family, Mom was naturally curious about the religion of her prospective son-in-law. An open-minded agnostic, she liked what she heard and remarked that if she were to have a religion, she thought it would be Native American because our spirituality was simple and grounded in the living creation.

Two years later, Mom asked, "Do you think it would be okay if I went to sweatlodge with you?" She really wanted to see for herself.

"Of course," I assured her.

The following Saturday night found her leaning against the outside of the lodge, listening intently to the ceremony inside. White-wolf, wary of subjecting a septuagenarian to the intense heat of the Inipi, placed her outside by the door keeper. She could listen safely from there. It was a cool, foggy night. Mom could not see fifty yards in front of her. In the distance, a kennel of howling dogs created a spooky atmosphere. She snuggled against the canvas lodge for protection against the eeriness and the evening's cold.

Then, inside she heard Whitewolf praying, "Oh Grandfather, we are honored to have this *old woman* sharing ceremony with us tonight."

With that, Mom stiffened a little.

"Grandfather, we appreciate having this *old woman* who is willing to come and learn something about our ways."

She set her jaw and squared her shoulders.

"Grandfather, we thank you for the old ones who have given us so much, and we thank you for this *old woman* outside the lodge who has taught her daughter the ways of respect and humility."

By this time, Mom was thoroughly irritated. After all, she wasn't that old. We explained later that being called an Old Woman was Whitewolf's way of honoring her. Being Old means being special. An Old Woman would know things. She had lived a long time.

Other than being slightly offended, Mom enjoyed the sweatlodge. It was a new experience for her and she loved the straightforward simplicity of it. We were not surprised later when Mom inquired, "Do you think I could go to another kind of ceremony?"

"Let's see." I called an acquaintance who not only keeps sweatlodge but also performs Lowanpi ceremonies. He invited us to attend Lowanpi the next weekend.

The Lowanpi ceremony is held in a special structure. It might be a room of a house or, as was this case, a cabin built specifically for that purpose. Lowanpi is a healing Sing Ceremony that lasts several hours. Once in the lodge, the doors are sealed and the windows shuttered and covered with light proof material so that it is pitch black inside. After the Lowanpi begins, no one can leave.

Mom and Priscilla sat with the women on one side of the lodge while I drummed and sang with the men on the other side. The Lowanpi was well underway with the drums driving their rhythm deep inside us. Mom could hear the medicine man in the center of his altar, when suddenly Spirit lights began to sparkle around the room. A host of lights danced around Mom and Priscilla as the Spirits announced their presence.

Mom was in awe. We had warned her not to analyze her experiences but to be present to them. Analysis could come later. She observed and absorbed the experience. In the pickup truck on the way home, she began to formulate a scientific understanding of what had occurred.

She hypothesized, "I think that, in the conditions of visual deprivation, the intense drumming must have stimulated the cerebral cortex and caused random retinal firing."

"Okay by me," I answered, not wanting to argue with her about it. After all, it didn't make a lot of difference how it happened. The amazing thing is that it happens at all.

That night we left Mom at her home, and Priscilla and I returned to Southern Maryland. The next morning as soon as her husband, Dave, headed for the laboratory, Mom, the true scientist, took two large pan lids and retreated to her bedroom closet. Shutting the door behind her, she scootched way back under her coats and on top of her shoes.

In the pitch darkness, she began to bang the lids together and chant, trying to replicate the experience of the night before. As she warmed to the task, the closet rocked with her efforts.

It sounded like someone being assaulted.

Unfortunately, Dave had forgotten his brief case. Irritated with his forgetfulness, he turned the car around and headed home. When he opened the front door, he was blasted by the yelling, banging, and screeching, all coming from the bedroom.

Dave raced down the hall in a panic, realized the noise was originating in the closet and yanked the door open just as Mom was poised for a fresh start.

What could he say to his bride of fifty years who was raising such a ruckus in the bedroom closet?

"What you are doing?" he demanded of his wife who now peered quietly up at him from the closet floor.

"Stimulating my cerebral cortex," she muttered, embarrassed, "To produce random retinal firing," she added.

Some years later, when Dave died, Mom came to live with us at age eighty-six. Three years earlier, she had been diagnosed with Alzheimer's disease. As is typical of many people with this affliction, Mom sometimes took to wandering. If we could not locate her in the house, we always knew where to find her. She and her devoted Sheltie would be outside in the woods, sitting by our sweatlodge. In good weather she returned there every day, sometimes sitting for hours in what had become her special place. Even without random retinal firings, she had found her spiritual home.

Mid-November

The tail of summer's warmth
Curled around us
On a full moon night;
The dogs howling,
The birds chattering,
The grasshoppers singing
In remembrance of languid August evenings.

Leafless oaks and resplendent pines
Striped the lawn, green and dark
Shadows, long and skinny,
Wisps of mist scattering
Moonlight into ghost light,
A moment of entry
For the little people.

Overhead, the white suns
Burned in a deep blue space
Scratched by white jet trails;
No sound, no red hot color,
The pale, silent stars
Stood watch
Over the earth's
Revolution,
North toward winter
South toward summer.

Last night, the sky
Gave up its gold and red
And fiery orange farewell
To the sun's retreat
And banked down
Into a silver glow.
The soft summer breeze
Chilled into the morning's
Grey light.

The dogs barked at the door;
The birds fluffed their wings;
The grasshoppers turned to stone;
And into the bleached, distilled air
The little people
Vanished.

—Priscilla Cogan

Full Circle

June 1989 – Sings-Alone's Place, Southern Maryland

O nce again my world was bounded by Vision Quest poles, colored flags, and tobacco ties. The afternoon sun bore into my skin. I shrank under a sliver of shade protecting the back edge of the altar. Hiding there in the shade, I pondered the past few years.

My pilgrimage had zig-zagged from the ministry through psychology to my native roots. When I had prayed for guidance before the statue of the Blessed Virgin, I had been led to search for my ancestors. Definitely a fool's journey, this had been my backwards path to God. In time, one man, Whitewolf, had emerged as my guide. He also had been my pivotal teacher through the mid-part of my travail.

Whitewolf was a beloved enigma. A patient, gentle, and devoted Elder, though younger than I, he was sometimes impetuous as an angry bull buffalo. His devotion to the people and the religion was as unshakable as his convictions about sacred matters. I absorbed from him an intense abhorrence of commercializing the religion or bastardizing the ceremonies. For seven years he was my educator, brother, and friend. Four or more weekly sweats were sandwiched between long, meandering conversations. His prayers protected me on the hill and his Spirit helpers interpreted my Visions. My debt to Whitewolf is incalculable.

When the time came to leave the safe nest of his camp, I was unable to make the break. Each time his camp gathered for a feast and celebration, he would announce that Sings-Alone was "leaving to establish his own camp and sweatlodge." When he finally gifted me an elaborately carved war club, I wryly observed, "Maybe this is the last warning and good-bye. I'd better go."

After departing from Whitewolf I established the Wild Potato Band, named for one of the original Cherokee Clans. I taught as I had been taught, and the Wild Potatoes flourished, but it was not quite enough. As I understood my task, I was to open a way for mixed-bloods to reconnect with their ancestors. The Wild Potato Band, despite its dedication, was too limited. We tried to unite with another established Cherokee group, but their purpose was to tap into government recognition and money. We connected with a second group, but found that they too wanted to use Indianess as a shortcut to a financial windfall. This preoccupation with riding Indian identity in the service of dollars was noxious to me.

A burning pain broke through my reverie. An ant served notice that I should be praying with my pipe. I vacated my shady refuge, knelt in the sun with the Sacred Pipe, and prayed for guidance. As Chief of the Wild Potato Band, I needed spiritual guidance.

Suddenly, the Grandfathers began to speak, "Gather your people into a tribe for assimilated Indians who yearn to come home. Let them be 'Free Cherokees.'"

Raising my pipe to the clouds, I said, "Hau, Grandfather! How do I do that?"

Only the breeze and the whispering pines responded. The Spirits love to tease me. There I sat, naked, in a Vision Quest alter being instructed to establish a Tribe of "lost" Indians. Ideally, it could facilitate many spiritual pilgrimages and be a bridge between the established tribes and their cousins. But it could just as easily degenerate into a front for New Age pseudo-Indian practices. Such a "tribe" could become the laughing stock of the Indian world

The Grandfathers, who love to play with my ego, had posed a daunting task for this Chief who at heart was an introvert. They at least could have counseled me about a structure for the Free Cherokees. Instead, they sent my furry friend to suggest, "No problem. Appoint some Chiefs. Invite independent bands to join up. Get membership cards. Folks like to flash them around pretending they mean something. Maybe you could sell Sacred Stoppers; big market there!"

After completing the final Vision Quest Sweat, I convened the Wild Potato Band Council and shared the Vision. To my relief, the Band unanimously accepted my sacred commission as its own. I invited a score of Indians to be Regional Chiefs for the Free Cherokees. Most accepted. Established bands and individuals enrolled in the Tribe. In a few years forty bands across the USA and Canada called themselves Free Cherokee. The Vision was growing.

The Tribe was a Coyote's delight. Some of the people were raised in an Indian culture. A few had learned some spiritual ways. Others, dressed in skins, feathers, and beads, tried to be Indian by playing Indian. Fortunately, most were eager to learn.

My reluctance and ambiguity as a national leader gnawed at me. I was a story-teller, Water Pourer, and teacher; not a politician. If the Free Cherokees were to thrive, Principal Chief Duncan Sings-Alone would have to step aside. And so, in May 1994 I became a Grandfather Chief, outside the loop of tribal government. Whatever the Free Cherokees would become lay squarely in the hands of the Chiefs and their Bands.

The Last Word . . . Maybe

December 1994 – Sings-Alone's place, Southern Maryland

Today, wrapped in a towel, eagle wing in hand, I called the Grandfather Spirits for a Sweatlodge Ceremony. A cool, winter breeze carried the call of my eagle bone whistle to the sky. Smoke from the sacred fire flavored the air. My heart surged in eager anticipation. Crouching, I entered the Lodge and crawled around the stone pit to my seat by the door. Longman, Gentle Spirit, and Priscilla followed. For now, this is the way I prefer to pray, surrounded by a small group of loved ones.

The lodge exuded the familiar musty smell of blankets long exposed to the elements. Settling down, cross-legged before the pit, I arranged my rattles, antlers, sage, sweetgrass, and cedar. Overhead, hung my Stoneman and tobacco ties. The eagle wing was at my side.

"Hokahey, Inyan!" I called for the red hot stones. One by one the Grandfather stones were brought by pitchfork and placed into the pit by our feet. Finally, the door keeper passed a bucket of water into the Lodge and sealed the flap. Home again, in the womb of Grandmother Earth, the deep blackness of the lodge formed a secure mantel around our shoulders. We sat quietly observing the stones, listening to them, waiting for a sign. Our knees and toes burned from the intense heat.

Ready at last, I sang my Spirit-Calling Song, and began to pour the water which burst into steam, licking our flesh in stinging delight. "Oh Grandfather above. My Grandfathers in all the Directions. Sky Beings. Grandmother Earth. This is your Grandson, Sings-Alone." The prayers began as they had hundreds of times before in the familiar sweatlodge litany. Peace flooded our hearts as we released the poisons and pettiness perverting our spirits.

Outside the Inipi's shelter, a new world was being born, a New Age of incredible spiritual chaos and hope. The Indian world continued to be ripped by fierce quarrels over who is a real Indian, and who has a right to ceremony in traditional ways. Labor pains are seldom pleasant.

Having followed the Spirits' directives to the best of my abilities, I yearned for quietness, for centering, and for healing a tired soul. It was and still is my time to sink into obscurity for a while.

But Coyote curls beside me resting for the next adventure. He is still watching, one eye open. . .or maybe in deep Zen meditation!

Mitakuye Oyas'in!

Glossary

Sacred Lakota Words and Descriptions

Hanblecheya—See Vision Quest

Inipi—See Sweatlodge

Inyan—Stones

Medicine—Spiritual power which may be used for healing, for Visions, and for making things happen. It may also be used for evil.

Medicine Animal—The Animal Spirit, not a specific animal, which can choose to work with a particular human being. Over time, an individual learns ways of knowing and acting unique to that species. The human being may take on the attributes of his/her animal Medicine. Animal Medicine often comes through Vision Questing.

Medicine bag—a small, buckskin pouch worn around the neck or on the belt. It contains sacred objects related to one's Vision.

Medicine Bundle—The Sacred Pipe, flat cedar, sage, sweet grass, tobacco, and items related to one's Medicine and Vision are kept wrapped in a small blanket or animal skin called the Sacred Bundle.

Medicine Man/Woman—An individual set apart by the creator, granted unusual spiritual power, and developed by a long apprenticeship to an established Medicine Person.

Medicine Teacher—Usually a person with a Sweatlodge and camp where sacred teachings are shared.

Medicine Wheel—A circle with cross bars in it. The wheel represents the Creation and the cross bars depict the four directions and the Spirits of those directions. Small medicine wheels the size of a silver dollar are cut from rawhide and decorated with porcupine quills. Eagle feathers may be attached to these and tied in the hair or on a hat band. These small medicine wheels are called quilled wheels.

Mitakuye Oyas'in—Phrase used in Lakota ceremonies to end prayers and sacred statements as "Amen" is used to close prayers in the Judeo-Christian tradition. Mitakuye Oyas'in means "All My Relations" referring to the entire creation: stones, rivers, trees, birds, four leggeds and fellow human beings of all races. By extension it refers to Oneness. Our prayers are made in all their names.

Pipe, Sacred—The Sacred Pipe (Chanunpa Wakan) was presented to human beings by the White Buffalo Calf Woman. It is the most revered ceremonial object, the altar in which sacred tobacco is burned.

Pipe Carrier—An individual who has demonstrated a long period of devotion to the religion and trained to provide Pipe Ceremony and other sacred rituals for his/her religious community.

Sacred Hoop—All of Creation: rocks, trees, waters, four-leggeds, fish, birds, crawling things, and human beings.

Sage—there are many varieties used as a ceremonial smudge or purifier. Some groups prefer Man Sage (artemisia silver queen). When sage leaves are rolled into a ball, they will smolder like incense. Sage smoke chases away unclean spirits and purifies the atmosphere. Flat cedar and sweet grass, often used with sage, invite Good Spirits to enter and do their work.

Stoneman—A small, sacred stone worn in a buckskin pouch around the neck.

Sweatlodge—The oldest known sacred ceremony on this continent. Sweatlodges in various forms are found in most tribes. The lodge mentioned in this book is an igloo shaped structure made of bent saplings and covered with blankets and canvass. The lodge is the womb of Grandmother Earth. In it the participants are purified, healed, and prepared to live in a good way. The Lodge is low to the ground so that one must crawl to enter. Once inside, participants sit around a shallow pit into which are placed stones heated to a glowing red. The Sweatlodge door is sealed, and water is poured on the stones. The ceremony is divided into four sections or rounds, each with its specific purpose. The lodge is very hot (one- hundred and forty to two-hundred degrees). The ceremony takes from one to three hours. This ritual should not be performed by untrained individuals. It can be physically dangerous.

Tobacco—The sacred herb used in prayers and ceremonies. A power herb, it is used in protected, circumscribed ways. Abused, it can destroy.

Tobacco Ties—Small cloth squares into which are folded pinches of tobacco. These are tied together on a string. Different ceremonies require varying numbers of tobacco ties. Tobacco ties carry the prayers of the participants.

Vision Quest—Also called "Hanblecheya" (Crying For a Vision)— A period of time from one to four days and nights in which a candidate prays and watches for a Vision while occupying a specially constructed altar area. The male candidate wears only a towel or Vision Quest skirt wrapped around his waist. The female quester wears a simple, light, cotton dress. No food or water is taken during the Vision Quest.

Vision Quest, Altar—The Vision Quest Altar affords the candidate a safe and sacred space in which to pray and watch for a Vision. The altar covers a square area no more than ten by ten feet. Each corner is marked by a freshly cut sapling and delineated by tobacco ties bearing the four direction colors. Within the Vision Quest space a smaller altar supports the Sacred Pipe.

Vision Quest, Hill—Sometimes the phrase, "Going on the hill", refers to a Vision Quest. Special hills are preferred for Vision Quest Altars. However, Hanblecheyas may occur anywhere selected by the candidate and his/her sponsor. Also used are special Vision pits in which the questers are buried for up to four days and nights.

Wakinyan—The Thunder Beings. They are identified with lightning and thunder.

Water Pourer—The Pipe carrier or Medicine person performing sweatlodge ceremonies.

Hymns Quoted

Chapter One   Maltbie D. Babcock. This Is My Father's World.

Chapter Two   John Fawcett. Blest Be The Tie That Binds.

Chapter Four   William Walford. Sweet Hour Of Prayer.

Chapter Five   Samuel Stone. The Church's One Foundation.

Postscript

D uncan Shoko Sings-Alone, a Grandfather Chief of the Free Cherokees and Priest/Roshi in the Zen Garland Order, lives in Massachusetts and Michigan with his wife, Priscilla Cogan, and two Shelties, Scamp and Rascal. All but Rascal are featured in this book. Sings-Alone divides his time between writing, and serving as spiritual director of Red Path Zen Sanghas in MI, MA, and NY. Priscilla is a novelist, poet, and Pipe Carrier. Her poetry graces this book.

We live in a Sacred World.

Mitakuye Oyas'in!
Roshi Duncan Shoko Sings-Alone